# BLACKTAIL DEER HUNTING ADVENTURES

## What others have said-

"Anyone who has ever hunted blacktail deer can relate to this book and can gain some good hunting lore from reading it. The book shows Wes's love and insight into this wonderful animal and the world it lives in." –Boyd Iverson (author of Blacktail Trophy Tactics)

"The technique is called 'still hunting,' and Murphey has learned to work it with enviable success. Blacktail Deer Hunting Adventures... promises to be well received by deer hunters." -- Mike Stahlberg (Eugene Register-Guard)

"I've read 'Blacktail Deer Hunting Adventures' with a great deal of interest and enjoyment. As a bow hunter who grew up hunting Whitetail deer, I know Murphey's methods for hunting blacktails can also be applied successfully to whitetails." –Rod Harder (Executive Director of Oregon Sportsmen's Defense Fund)

"Very well done!" –Dan Poynter (Author of The Self-Publishing Manual)

*Pleasant reminders of past hunts*

# BLACKTAIL
# DEER HUNTING
# ADVENTURES

A Refreshingly Candid Account
Valuable For Hunters Everywhere

Wesley Murphey

LOST CREEK BOOKS
Eugene, Oregon

# BLACKTAIL DEER HUNTING ADVENTURES

Published by:   Lost Creek Books
PO Box 50185
Eugene, OR 97405

Publishing consultation provided by
Vesta Publishing Services, Eugene, OR

Printed by McNaughton and Gunn, Inc.

Printed on recycled paper

**Copyright © 1995** by Wesley S. Murphey

Cover design: Howard Rooks
Cover photos: Oregon Dept. of Fish and Wildlife
Typeset/Layout: Don Bowers, Wes Murphey
Illustrations: Don Murphey, John Murphey, Ryan Sather

Library of Congress Catalog Card Number 94-76671

ISBN 0-9641320-4-4

Non-fiction
1. Deer Hunting
2. Deer Hunting Adventure
3. Outdoor Adventure

Printed in the United States of America

# BLACKTAIL DEER HUNTING ADVENTURES

## CONTENTS

# ACKNOWLEDGMENTS

I would like to thank the following people for their contributions to the writing of this book in the form of material, information and encouragement: Mark Adkins; Ken Byford (Willamette National Forest); Dick Savage, Li Scheng; Rod Harder of Oregon Sportsmen's Defense Fund; my brother John Murphey and Ryan Sather for their cartoons; my sister Carla Joy Murphey-Andelt for her editorial feedback on a portion of my early draft; The following Oregon Department of Fish and Wildlife personnel: Tony Burtt, Herman Biederbeck, Dick Irish, Randy Henry, Tom Thornton and others.

Special thanks to Trudy Kutz, Eugene Bible College English Professor, for editing my final manuscript; my dad, Don Murphey, for much editorial feedback, drawings and constant encouragement; Howard Rooks for cover design and paste up of photos and drawings; Don Bowers, Director of Computer Services at Eugene Bible College, for computer typesetting and layout work; Gwen Rhoads, Vesta Publishing Services, Inc. for consultation; and Kaycie Galdabini (photo copy work) and John Miller (photo screening) of Central Print and Blueprint.

I also thank my many hunting partners and the other people named in the book but not mentioned above.

# BLACKTAIL DEER HUNTING ADVENTURES

## INTRODUCTION

How many deer hunting articles or books have you read over the years that were introduced with a relatively short hunting adventure which you were immediately drawn in to and in which you at once identified with the hunters involved, only to be disappointed to find that the author's description of the hunt ended as quickly as it had begun? The author had then proceeded to talk about deer habits, deer habitat, places to hunt, and various methods of successfully hunting deer, just like so many other authors before him had done. Certainly you enjoyed reading what each author shared on these topics, and learned from them, but like me, you were left to wonder why so many authors of deer hunting writings did not tell you about more of their hunting adventures.

BLACKTAIL DEER HUNTING ADVENTURES was written with the specific goal of giving hunters the opportunity to read about and enjoy many different deer hunting adventures. The adventures in this book are a very representative sample of my own blacktail hunting experiences written in a chronological narrative form, beginning with the taking of my first deer. I have included the hunts each year in which I filled my deer tag or tags, as well as numerous other hunts in which I took part. The hunting adventures included in this book give the reader a good taste of West Coast blacktail deer hunting.

Throughout the narrative and in several separate chapters I have included many hunting tips and discussed topics of interest to *all deer hunters*. Most of the ideas and opinions expressed in this book are based on my own hunting experiences and observations. Some people will undoubtedly disagree with me on some points. But I hope all readers will agree that Blacktail Deer Hunting Adventures is a candid account, unique in its presentation, and valuable to hunters everywhere no matter what species of deer they pursue.

*(Willamette National Forest Photo)*

# TWO GREAT LOVES

Submerged deep beneath the Pacific Ocean's surface, miles from land, I day-dreamed of being back home in Oregon's woods where I spent so many of my boyhood hours. Finally, in April 1979 my dream was realized when I completed my four-year hitch in the Navy, the last three and a half having been spent aboard the nuclear-powered fast-attack submarine USS Guardfish SSN-612 as an enlisted navigation specialist (Quartermaster). I returned home to Oregon's Willamette Valley with great aspirations and tremendous enthusiasm.

As a kid I lived in Dexter, Oregon, located about twelve miles southeast of Eugene, from my sixth through twelfth grade years of school. Living in a small rural community like Dexter, where I had ready access to the nearby woods and mountains in addition to Dexter Lake, Lost Creek, and the Willamette River, melded well with my innate love for the outdoors and particularly the forest. I loved anything having to do with the wild, including swimming, camping, fishing, hunting, and hiking. In our early teen years, my twin brother Rob and I, along with our friends Tim Mole and Jay Lohner, called ourselves "The Mount Zion Adventurers." Our favorite slogan was "Zion or Bust!" indicative of our insatiable desire to conquer Mount Zion, a peak of 2,625 feet, overlooking Dexter and the Lost Creek valley.

The bulk of my early hunting experience was bird hunting with my M-I carbine style BB gun. In high school I took Dad's twelve-gauge shotgun out deer hunting a couple of years, and one year I used my step-mother's 300 Savage. However, I never saw a buck in the woods during deer season before I went into the service. Little did I know back then that after I got out of the Navy I would take an exceptional liking to deer hunting, eventually becoming a successful blacktail hunter.

Before telling of the experience of shooting my first buck, I must say that during the winter season of my senior year of high school, 1974-75, I contracted a disease which would prove to be incurable. Though I had been exposed regularly to the virus at home until I was five years old and again, superficially, during my junior year, I hadn't fallen prey until that senior year. Because of seasonal regulations, this disease is forced into remission for six or seven months a year. However, once the days get shorter, the nights cooler, and the air damper in mid-fall, this affliction prevails upon me again. As many of my friends and peers know, this disease is called fur trapping. Only another trapper can truly appreciate my love for the sport. Dad got me hooked while teaching me the ropes on his trapline during my last winter as a boy before Uncle Sam got me.

Trapping and blacktail deer hunting have many similarities, as well as some differences. Both are done in many types of weather. Both require observation, analysis, and skill. And both are loaded with anticipation. A big difference is that most often in trapping, the buildup in excitement comes at very pre-dictable times—immediately prior to checking each trap. With deer hunting the excitement can come at any time during the day. Trapping provides many small thrills, as opposed to the fewer large ones of deer hunting. In trapping, there is always tomorrow—but not in deer hunting. An opportunity missed on a big buck will rarely present itself again.

I love hunting and trapping, largely because I am pitted against my quarry in their own environment—a place that is exhilarating to me. I am constantly learning more about the animals I pursue as well as their environment. I truly enjoy wild animals, but I also know that they eventually die by one means or another and that my having a part in that event does not make me immoral or inhuman. Wild animals must be man-aged, and if man doesn't manage them, nature will do so in a much less humane manner using predation, disease, and star-vation as its primary tools. For men to benefit from various animal and plant species' existence while being conscientious enough to ensure their healthy perpetuation is good steward-ship of natural resources. I believe it is the way God intended.

When I harvested my first deer, a desire was stirred from deep within me to take part annually in the pruning of Oregon's blacktail deer population. Blacktail deer, like the furbearing animals I trap, are one of Oregon's abundant renewable resources. I'm very thankful that in this country and specifically in this state, I have the right and the opportunity to pursue one of my greatest loves—Blacktail Deer Hunting.

*Wes getting after the beaver.*

# FALL 1979
# A HALLOWEEN INITIATION

Wednesday, October 31st, 1979, Halloween day. My older sister Becky's birthday was the day before on the 30th, but until 1979 I could never remember whether her birthday or Halloween came first. Somehow, when I punched out the date on that first deer tag, many events that day were etched into my mind forever.

I was attending Eugene Bible College as a freshman and had gone out deer hunting on Saturdays and on numerous afternoons. Being the rookie hunter I was, I had jumped only a few deer all season and only seen one. That's hard to believe now. I had so much to learn about blacktail deer. I must confess that sometimes, even now, after hunting a day or two without seeing any deer, I wonder if I really know much about blacktails.

That year, October 31st was the first of the final five days of the general blacktail season when a hunter could shoot any deer he saw—a so-called Hunter's Choice Season. The weather was dry and mild. After getting home from school and eating a quick lunch shortly after noon, I grabbed the Remington 30.06 auto-loader which I had borrowed for the season and headed up to Lookout Point Reservoir on the Middle Fork of the Willamette River above Lowell, fifteen miles southeast of Eugene along Highway 58. I drove clear up to the top of School Creek Road, which meets the North Shore Road twelve miles above Lowell, and did some still-hunting (moving along slowly while hunting) in a couple of different stands of timber. Finally, late in the afternoon, I stopped alongside a reprod unit of ten-to twelve-year-old firs bordered by old-growth and large second-growth Douglas Fir on three sides. ("Reprod unit" is short for "reproduction unit," a unit that has been logged of large timber and replanted.) It was a spot I had never hunted before. After walking around in the thick reprod unit for half an hour, I had the thought, "Maybe I won't get a deer this year!"

With what little hope I could muster, I decided to go into the large timber bordering the south side of the young growth, an area perhaps 200 yards from the road I had parked on. It was around 4:45 pm and the day was quickly coming to a close. When I reached the tall firs, I slowly moved along deeper into the shade and down a slightly sloping ridge. Twenty minutes later I heard a blue jay squawk below me, immediately gaining my attention. A good friend and accomplished hunter, Orv Stephens, had told me earlier in the season that often a blue jay will warn of a deer's movement. Since then, I've learned that a jay will sound off at any movement, especially a man's. Squirrels can also be a nuisance at times in this regard.

Moments later I heard a limb snap, confirming the fact that an animal, probably a deer, was headed up the steep side of the ridge, below and to my left. Within seconds a pair of deer trotted into view. Instantly my heart-rate accelerated. As they came up the ridge moving away from me and to my right, I realized that I needed to change position to get a clear shot. Easing the safety off my weapon, I took a few slow, quiet steps to my right, positioning myself where I felt I would have the best opportunity for an open shot between the big fir trees. The lead deer crossed too quickly, but the second one stopped momentarily on a small, coffin-sized knoll about fifty yards from me, with its nose high in the air, and sniffed the wind. With the light growing dimmer by the minute in the big timber and the deer's head tipped back toward me, I did not immediately discern if the deer had antlers, though its body was large. Antlers didn't matter anyway, because I could legally shoot any deer I saw. As the deer stood quartered away from me with its head high in the air, I quickly aimed for its neck and fired. At the sound of my shot I saw legs sticking in the air, and I knew I had connected. I ran the short distance and was thrilled to see the deer was a tight-racked four by three blacktail buck. I yelled, "Thankyou God!" several times, jumping up and down and throwing a fist in the air. The euphoria of that moment for me has only been matched by two other experiences in my whole life—those were being present at the births of my two children, Cody Scott and Tasha Lynn.

Seeing that four-point buck lying there on the moss-covered ground was like a miracle! The fact that it was a four-point was important too in its own way, since my oldest brother Bill's first deer was also a four-point. I must concede, though, that his buck's rack was much more impressive, sporting four points and double eye guards on each antler. Also, Bill was only a fifteen-year-old boy at the time, in 1966, whereas I had to wait until I was twenty-two for my first buck. (When counting antler points on blacktails and mulies out West the common method is to count the number of points on the side with the most points—excluding the "eye guards" or "brow tines" if present. Therefore a buck with three points on one side and only two on the opposite side would be called a three point regardless of whether either or both sides had eye guard points. In the East a whitetail-deer hunter counts the total of every point on both sides. As a result the three by two buck just mentioned would be called a five point. If it also had brow tines it would be a seven pointer.)

After the buck stopped kicking, I proudly pulled out my deer tag and tore off the Oct and 31 before tying the tag around an antler. I continued to admire my buck as I contemplated the task of gutting it and getting it out to the car which was about 400 yards away. Although I had cleaned hundreds of cold fish, I had never gutted out a large warm-blooded animal. (Being a veteran now of many guttings, it seems funny that I hesitated on that first deer.) I debated trying to get the buck to the car without gutting it, but after attempting to lift it, I knew that wasn't feasible. Daylight was slipping away fast now, so I pulled out my pocket knife and went to work. The innards out, I crawled into position where I could drape the deer across my shoulders in a fireman's carry. Strenuously, I got to my feet, picked up my rifle, and slowly hiked to the car. What a load!

How little preparation I had that first year. Looking back, I see that many times over the years I could have saved a lot of work, discomfort, and time by using my head better. Of course, packing out any adult buck is hard work. Nonetheless, most hunters have the advantage of killing their first deer while hunt

ing with someone else who can also help get it out. Admittedly, my adrenalin level from my excitement was at an all-time high, which aided my task.

By the time I reached the car with the deer, it was pitch dark. I had lain down with the deer to rest a couple times. On the drive down the mountain and down the North Shore Road to Lowell, I almost wrecked the car three times, barely pulling out of the ditch each time. I wanted to show my deer off and couldn't get out fast enough.

I stopped at my long-time friend Ruby Hensley's place (first house below Lookout Point Dam) to call Dad. At Dad's place, my step-mother, Rosella, answered the phone. When I told her that I got a four-point buck, she responded, "Oh, you did not." She was joking, of course, but due to my excitement, I actually started crying. I told her to let me talk to Dad. Emotions certainly can be unpredictable. Rosella was glad for me and believed me, I'm sure. Anyway, after talking to Dad and showing my buck to Ruby and her husband, Curt (a very good hunter himself), I made several stops at other friends' houses to show off my buck. Eventually, I arrived at Dad's to skin and care for the deer.

Thus the christening of the great and avid—avid at least—blacktail hunter, Wes Murphey!

When hunting throughout that first season following my military tour, I really didn't know if I was doing anything right because I had no previous success on which to base my decisions and actions. Over the years, I have learned a lot from mistakes I made that cost me deer in addition to what I gleaned from the times I killed deer.

I believe the two most important factors in becoming a consistently successful blacktail hunter are (1) spending lots of time in the woods where the deer are, and (2) taking notes, mentally and otherwise, on the many observations made while afield. In other words, spend time in nature's classroom and pay attention to nature's teachers.

Although blacktails are not very predictable, they do have definite preferences and tendencies that can be exploited to their detriment. Learning the most likely times and places to see deer will certainly cut down on the amount of hunting time "wasted" in less productive areas. For example, large bucks might be found in clearcuts at first light on opening morning or even on other days during the season if there is (1) slight hunting pressure, and (2) protective cover in the form of benches, ravines, brush or trees within a few feet. Otherwise, forget it! Any legal bucks that are foolish enough to be in the open when hunters are prowling about won't live long enough to ever be a large buck. Of course, there are rare exceptions. Sometimes a buck will bed in a clearcut if he is well concealed and can make a safe get-away down a draw, etc., should the need arise. Knowing that big bucks will, however, often feed in openings until shortly before dawn and then make their way to their beds not far away when the day breaks affords the resourceful hunter the opportunity to set up an ambush on the appropriate deer trail in the timber bordering the clearcut.

*Wes's first deer - a beauty!*

# FALL 1980
# A SAD MISTAKE

Before getting to the event of my second buck's demise, I want to make a confession. Somehow, in my mind, I felt that I was already an accomplished hunter after that first buck. However, the next season, 1980, proved to me the futility of my thinking.

On opening day, my house-mate and fellow Bible College student, Steve (whose last name I won't mention because of what happened), my twin brother Rob, and I went hunting up Goodman Creek on the south side of Lookout Point Reservoir. It was October 4th, and the weather had been very dry and hot for several days. In fact, only two days earlier, on the 2nd, the temperature reached ninety-four degrees setting a new record for the date. On this day the temperature reached into the low eighties by mid-afternoon. Hunting conditions were poor as the woods were very dry.

We hunted all morning, working some creeks, draws and ridges, without seeing so much as a single deer. Nonetheless, I did find a shed three-point antler. Finding an antler periodically while hunting is one of the subtle payoffs and inspirations of the sport for me. On several occasions I have found more than one antler in the same day.

Our morning's fruitless hunting efforts, nevertheless, had burned off our breakfast calories, so we returned to Steve's '73 Chevy Blazer to eat. But as luck had it, we had managed to leave our lunch on the table at home. Fortunately, you might say, Steve had some Dexatrim tablets in his glove compartment, so we each popped a couple. Since neither Rob nor I were trying to lose weight, going hungry and dropping diet pills didn't fit into our original game plan. Nowadays, I know of a number of edible wild plants to feed on if necessary. At that time, though, I only knew of a few plants and mushrooms. We did find some sorrel which we ate sparingly.

Early in the afternoon, we split up and hunted a sloping unit of second-growth fir and hemlock. About thirty minutes after parting, I heard a single gunshot from a couple hundred yards up the hill behind me to the southeast. I shouted, "Did you get one?" but got no answer. I then worked toward the shot's direction, knowing Rob and Steve were up that way, and yelled again.

Steve hollered back, "I got a five-point!" Immediately, I stepped up my pace as I was anxious to see his trophy buck. In the process, I jumped a deer but I couldn't make out antlers in the shade of the woods. I debated going after the deer, which was headed in the opposite direction from where Steve had yelled, but instead, I gave in to the urge to see Steve's big buck. Boy, was I going to be surprised.

When I came into sight of Steve, I saw that he and Rob were together, but something wasn't right. They seemed downcast rather than excited. It turned out that the buck Steve shot was a spike—an illegal deer—rather than a five-point. (In Western Oregon's General Blacktail Season a buck must have at least one forked antler in order to be legally taken.) We didn't know what to do, whether to report the dead deer or try to sneak it out. The heat of the day was certainly a factor. Ironically, Steve's two favorite phrases—which both Rob and I readily adopted into our own vocabularies due to Steve's enthusiastic use of them—were, "That's trick!" and "No doubt!" If only Steve had had some doubt before pulling the trigger and killing the spike, we wouldn't have ended up in such a bind. After a minute of strained silence, and a few more spent discussing our options, Steve and I decided to pray about it. Upon opening our eyes from praying, we immediately noticed a couple of bald-faced hornets inspecting the dead deer. Steve had prayed for a sign and, because he was allergic to bee stings, we took the hornets presence as our cue. As a result, we left the stag lay and hiked out to the rig to hunt somewhere else. On the drive out we were stopped by a pair of game wardens, who checked our licenses. We would have been hung out to dry if we had kept the deer or even gutted it.

I've learned the hard way since then, via a trapping incident in which I overlooked a call-in deadline on a *legally* caught bobcat, that the law does not forgive accidental kills or other incidental oversights, no matter how minor. My oversight cost me a bobcat pelt and netted me forty hours of community service. (Originally I was ordered to pay $350 restitution.)

When Steve killed that deer, I thought, "I would never make that kind of mistake." Yet, a few years later, I did make a similar error, painfully reminding me of the old adage, "One should never say, 'It can't happen to me!'" Even the most experienced hunter can find himself in a compromising situation if he gives in to the adrenalin rush that so often accompanies the sighting of a deer in the woods during deer season. The only sure way to avoid such a mistake is to refuse to pull the trigger unless you are absolutely positive of what you are seeing.

The hunter who mistakenly shoots a doe or spike because of "buck fever" will carry remorse for his error for some time, but not like the hunter who shoots another human while hunting. That hunter will bear the weight of his error forever. Tragically, an occasional hunter or hiker does get shot by a hunter because he is mistaken for a deer or other game, or because he is in the background of game being shot at. Certainly the prudent hunter or hiker will not wear white, brown, gray, or black clothing in the woods during big game hunting seasons because those colors match the colors of popular large game animals. Moreover, the outdoorsman can greatly improve his odds for safety by wearing highly visible clothing colored in blaze-orange or red. I typically wear a red and black plaid shirt and hat, though on rare occasions I use camouflaged clothing.

Some state's have laws mandating hunters to wear blaze-orange colored clothing while in the field. At present, Oregon has no such law, though some legislators have recently pushed for such a restriction. Needless to say, anyone who chooses to hunt—as with any other sport—is accepting whatever risks come with the activity and should have the freedom to choose the color and type of clothing he wants to wear. Considering the number of hunters (over 300,000), and the number of hours they spend hunting each year in Oregon, the accident rate is very low. Furthermore, most of the accidents that do occur while hunting—such as someone discharging a weapon while getting in or out of a vehicle —would not be prevented even if blaze-orange clothing were worn. (I have included some specific data on firearms accidents in the chapter "Hunting Accidents.")

During the 1980 season, Steve and I hunted together on several more occasions, including a couple times in the Willamette Unit, northwest of Eugene, in November. We seemed to work pretty well together as to pace of hunt and instincts. We also had a lot of laughs. However, I have done far more hunting alone and prefer it, as I can be totally flexible. One definite plus to hunting with others is that one has someone to talk with on the drive home or in camp and at various times throughout the day. Being able to chat with a partner about aspects of the hunt, such as determining hunting strategies and assessing hunts, is particularly enjoyable to me. There is no doubt that hunting partners who know the lay of the land and work well together can in the right circumstances—such as when it is extremely dry or the deer are bedded—have better luck than a solo hunter. Many hunters much prefer to hunt with other people rather than by themselves, I believe, because for them hunting is more of a social activity. Maybe I choose to hunt alone because I take my deer hunting more seriously—maybe too seriously at times.

Although I jumped and saw a number of deer during the 1980 season, not one was a shootable buck. Additionally, when hunting during the Hunter's Choice portion of the General Deer Season and a few times in the November Willamette Unit Hunter's Choice Season—when I could have shot any of the does I saw early on—I did not even manage to get my sights on a doe, which I would have gladly shot for some meat. Result: I never fired a shot. I did lots of hiking, had lots of disappointment and lots of fun, and, yes, I learned a lot. It was an enjoyable deer season, but one that showed me how difficult it can be to see a blacktail buck and, at times, even a doe, let alone shoot one. My good friend and fellow Bible College student, John Christenson, also a deer hunting fanatic, who had listened enthusiastically a year earlier as I shared my hunting success story, returned the favor when he related the story of harvesting his first deer ever—a doe—during Hunter's Choice. John also gave me half of the deer's meat, while donating the other half to Eugene Bible College. He lived on campus and ate his meals in the college cafeteria.

A very nice blacktail buck  (ODFW Photo)

# FALL 1981
# FOOLISH OLD BUCK

Opening morning, October 3rd, Steve and I hunted the backside of the burned hill at milepost eleven on the North Shore Road at Lookout Point Reservoir. We had hunted there the year before and had seen a number of non-legal deer. Before daylight, I hiked up the old skid road which went up hill to the west, bordered by second-growth fir on the left and a canyon with ten-year-old reprod firs on the right. I was carrying a used Remington model 742 semi-automatic 30.06 with a Bushnell 3X9 variable scope, which Dad had given to me as a gift during the previous summer. Steve hiked up the north side of the reprods to my right, following along the timberline of large firs there.

A spring ran through the middle of the replanted unit in the brush-choked canyon. This area provided excellent habitat for blacktails because there was a great mixture of large second-growth and old-growth fir, maple, oak and alder trees. In the bottom there were also some willows along the spring. Blackberry bushes, which deer take a special liking to, were thick in places in the canyon as well. Neither Steve or I had hunted this spot at daylight, so we were optimistic. We had gotten up especially early in order to be sure to be the first hunters there, and we were.

At first light, I came into the grassy field area to my left laying 200 yards up the steep hill and to the south of the older reprod unit on my right. To the south of the field was a prime hunting hillside of sparse four-to six-year-old firs. Between me and the hillside was a draw with fairly thick brush and a number of young maple trees in their yellow fall colors, that were scant enough to not interfere with my view of the hill. The area with the young fir trees also had an assortment of fern, scotch-broom, and grass, and spotty patches of blackberries. The angle and view for scoping were great, and I immediately spotted a doe and a spike watching me as they stood a third of the way up the hill about seventy-five yards away. As hard as I tried, I could not see a fork on either of the young buck's ant-lers, so I could only watch.

One thing I have learned about any reprod unit with mixed vegetation is that deer blend in extremely well. Besides that, they can be bedded out of sight or be standing behind some brush. Shaded areas are particularly difficult to critique, which is one reason why I prefer that the sun not be shining when I hunt. When hunting the open, I like a mist with overcast skies, while in the timber I prefer a light drizzle with minimal or no breeze. On sunny days a hunter is much easier for game to spot, whereas for the hunter, animals are harder to see. On less bright days I can see into shady areas much more easily. Another advantage to overcast days is that I don't have any problems with glare to my optics—rifle scope or binoculars. I carry my binocs with me almost all the time, even in the timber, because they allow me to see detail much better. For example, I've spotted a deer's motionless ear through brush at thirty yards using binoculars when I would never have seen it other-wise. I've also located a number of bedded deer that I hadn't seen with my un-aided eyes.

After several minutes, the doe and spike I had been watching got nervous and sneaked away, finally going over the ridge out of my sight. I gradually moved farther up the grass field, glassing the hillside as I went. Though the weather had been dry, the knee-high grass was damp from the night's dew, so I could move very quietly. The wind was blowing out of the west, the direction I was hunting. Quietly I hiked past a little cove near the top of the field, and when I was about thirty yards beyond it, a buck jumped up from the cover. He must have been bedded in the cove and winded me when I got past him, but instead of remaining hidden he foolishly ran into the open. Instinctively, I turned toward the deer, and seeing he had a wide rack, I took a quick shot at his rib-cage as he trotted to my right, broadside to me at twenty-five yards. When he continued trot-ting, I again pulled on the trigger, but the gun didn't fire as I had inadvertently engaged the safety. By the time I was ready for another shot, the branch-antlered buck had kicked it into running gear and was going straight away from me toward the ridge to the south. I aimed for the the back of his head, which was the only good target I had, and shot when he was about sixty yards away, at the ridge. He disappeared! I didn't know if he had cleared the crest of the hill or gone down. Hustling over, I found him lying in the thigh-high grass on the ridge line. It was eight a.m.. The old buck, a gnarly-antlered forked-horn with an eighteen-inch inside spread, was obviously well past his prime as evidenced by his completely gray face, badly worn teeth, and antlers. His right antler was deformed from having been injured while in the velvet stage of development. I yelled for Steve, who arrived several minutes later and subsequently helped get the deer down the hill. The meat from that deer proved to be quite tough, though flavorful. I'm sure that part of the meat's toughness could be attributed to my not aging it properly.

After getting my buck on opening morning, I still made an effort to get into the field as much as possible during the remainder of the deer season in order to add to my growing knowledge of blacktail deer.

*Cody Murphey (1994) with antlers from his
dad's forked horn killed in 1981*

# FALL 1982
# ACE IN THE HOLE

During my senior year of Bible college I hunted whenever I could, but because I was working Thursdays to Saturdays at the Canned Foods Store in Glenwood, my opportunities for morning hunts were very limited.

After class one warm dry afternoon in mid-October I was hunting above a huge clearcut to the north of Lookout Point's North Shore Road. The terrain there was quite steep, with most of the hillside being steeper than thirty-five degrees. I was on the south-facing side of the mountain (the side facing the reservoir), where old growth and large second-growth Douglas firs were the staple. In addition there were numerous large cedar trees, some hemlock and grand fir, and smatterings of alder, oak, big-leaf maple, and vine maple. Along the rockiest areas, madrone, chinqapin, and "scrub oak" were abundant. This mixture of tree species is typical in western Oregon's Douglas fir forests. A person stranded in the woods can get sustenance from many of these trees at various times of the year. The nuts on oak and chinquapin ripen in late summer, while madrone berries ripen in early fall. Maple syrup can be obtained from the maple's sap when it is running in the spring and early summer. Additionally, many of the evergreen species' needles can be used to make tea year round. Mature evergreen trees also yield cones which contain edible nuts, though the large pine-cones are best for this. So many foods are available in the wild. Add to the plants all the edible animals and insects, and one can have quite a smorgasbord, as the American Indians well knew. Of course, some wild foods are very tasty while others, though edible, would rate as poor table fare. The method of preparation is important in making some foods, like acorns, palatable. Certainly, one should never eat a wild plant unless he is positive of its identity as well as its edibility. Even a small bite of some poisonous plants can be fatal.

While hiking up through the clearcut below, I hadn't seen or scared any deer, nor had I done so in the two hours I had been working along sidehill to the east in the timber, some 200 yards above the cleared unit. My brother Bill had come up here hiking with a friend a day or so earlier and had told me he had seen a five-point buck near the overhangs and rock cliffs that are prevalent along the upper reaches of this stretch of mountains. Bill's mention of seeing a trophy buck—whether exaggerated or not—had stirred my interest in hunting the cliff area.

When I was just reaching the long, sloping ridge extending south to my right, a beautiful, wide-antlered buck jumped up out of its bed not thirty feet to my right and ran straight across in front of me. Instantly, I released the safety and shouldered my .06 in one motion. I was on the deer's body at once, but where? All I could see was dark-gray buck hair, so I didn't pull the trigger. Following the hair to the left with my scope, I was about to shoot when the deer disappeared behind a four-foot-wide fir tree about thirty yards away. Continuing my rifle-swing past the big tree, I figured I'd get a shot when the buck got past it. Unfortunately, when the buck got the tree between us, he ran straight away and down over the bank, not giving me another look. I nearly cried! Immediately, I looked at the scope setting and found it to be on five power, instead of the three setting I always use in timber. I had forgotten to turn my scope back down after walking up through the clearcut below. A big buck, running broadside to me at very close range, and in my sights for over two seconds, had lived because of a mistake I had made two hours earlier. I could not have asked for a better opportunity for a clear, close-range shot, but on that day fate was on the side of that mossy-back buck.

About a week later, on a cool Sunday morning I returned to the area up School Creek where I had bagged my first buck three years earlier. Getting there just before daylight, I hiked back to the timbered ridge of my previous good fortune. Hunting slowly and quietly along the west edge of the ridge, I decided to sit down and watch the ridge area to the south of me for a while. Since it was quite cool out at that elevation, it wasn't long before I had to move out of the cold west wind just to keep from shaking.  So I walked down over the east side of the ridge just enough to get out of the wind and looked the steep hill-side below me over as best I could.  That side of the hill sloped at over forty-five degrees, though there was a small grassy flat over a hundred yards below me to my left.

After five minutes, around 8:45, I chose to sit down so I could comfortably watch below me.  Since there were some sticks in my way, I laid my rifle down a few feet away and began quietly getting the sticks out of my seating area.  As I lifted the fourth stick, a very nicely antlered buck exploded from his bed about twenty yards below me.  I instantly dropped the stick and grabbed my rifle, but unfortunately the buck was wasting no time bouncing down the hill to my left.  The big trees and the steep grade interfered with my chances for a shot, but finally as the buck slowed to a trot near the grassy knoll, I did get a shot off, aimed right between his shoulder blades.  At that point, he was 100 yards distant.  When my gun recoiled, I lost sight of him, and thinking I had connected, I hustled down to where I had last seen him.  He was not to be found in the near vicinity, nor did I find blood.  Most likely, I missed over him.  However, in retrospect, I believe that I did not look around the whole area as well as I should have.  Since then I've learned a lot more about how to determine if a hit is made on an animal and also how to track animals.  Two of the biggest keys in tracking game are to be systematic in searching for sign and then to stay off it once it is found.

That big buck had held tight in his bed after undoubtedly winding me for probably fifteen minutes and hearing me for at least five.  Over the years since then I've learned that this is S.B.O.P. (standard blacktail operating procedure).  How many big bucks have I walked right by while they watched me from their beds?  Several times I have gotten a brief glimpse of deer sneaking quickly away through the woods without making a sound.  In some cases, the only reason I even saw them sneaking away was because I had sensed their presence and just happened to look in their direction.  I wonder how many deer have sneaked away that I didn't hear or see?  Interestingly, I have observed many does and fawns that upon seeing me have tip toed away, lifting their legs high as they quietly picked their way through downed limbs and brush right out in plain sight of me. Never have I seen a large old, branch-antlered buck behave this way. The reason, of course, is that any buck inclined to make that kind of error would not have survived to be old.

I believe certain survival techniques displayed by deer have been genetically passed down from offspring to offspring, whereas some have been learned through successful past encounters with predators and man. Additionally, young deer observe the behavior of older deer and learn to respond the same way in various situations. On the other hand, I don't believe that deer go through any kind of cognitive process when confronted with danger, but rather, they simply react according to

the way their brains have been previously programmed. In other words, a deer doesn't think, "If I lie here in the ferns, he'll walk right past me and never know I'm here." Or, "I smell a hunter, so I think I'll sneak out of here before he gets close enough to catch me [rather than shoot me]; I think my best bet is to go lie down in the dense vine maple thicket that Uncle Buck uses when he senses danger."

I know there are those who totally disagree with my thinking on this, including some hunters and many animal rightists. Certainly, anybody who believes that Disney's "Bambi" even remotely presents the reality of how wild animals think and communicate would take exception to my opinion here. For the record, I do like Disney's movies.

Before dawn on the next to last day of Hunter's Choice, which was only three days long that year, I returned to the huge clearcut across from the gravel pit on Lookout Point Reservoir's North Shore Road. I had seen a number of antlerless deer throughout the buck-only season preceding Hunter's Choice but didn't see any deer while hunting after class the previous afternoon, the first day of the Choice season. Just after daybreak, as the sun's light crept down the top of the fir-covered mountain to my north, I slowly advanced up the gated-off, dirt logging road running up the middle of the year-old clearcut. While scanning the area above me to the left of the road, I noticed two does looking at me as they stood frozen 125 yards away, presenting only a straight-on profile to me. Because of the ditch on the edge of the dirt road, I couldn't get to a stump to rest my rifle. I cranked my scope up to about six power and debated on chancing an off-hand shot. I don't like off-hand shots of that distance when all I have to aim at is a deer's chest. Nonetheless, instead of waiting for the deer to get nervous and turn to the side where I would have a better target, I gave into my poorer judgment and aimed at the center of the left deer's chest and pulled the trigger. At my shot, two more does jumped up and joined the first two in a brush-busting run to the left. I promptly emptied the other four shells from my auto-loading 30.06 in the fleeting deers' direction but got no encouragement from the deer for my efforts. Quickly, I jacked the clip out of my weapon, reloaded it, and replaced it. By then the deer had run over the top of the ridge out of my sight, so I ran up to where the first one had stood and looked for any sign of a hit. Finding none, I searched along the route the deer had taken over the mostly dirt covered ground, but found neither blood or any dead deer. Had one of the deer been killed, I would have easily found it as the vegetation was very sparse. That was the only time I've fired more than three shots at a deer. I found out that day how difficult it can be to hit a hard-running deer that is even a moderate distance away.

I ended up not getting a deer the rest of that day or the next one, which ended the regular season, adding to my remorse over bungling my earlier opportunities on those two big bucks. Basically I had conceded that I was done for the year because the only unit still open for rifle hunters was the Willamette Unit, where I found very little public land when looking for a place to hunt out there in 1980.

Then on November 24th, the day before Thanksgiving, I was sitting in the cafeteria at Eugene Bible College telling a friend, Betty Gibson, that I hadn't gotten my deer, when she mentioned that they see deer on their place. All of a sudden it dawned on me that they owned land in the Willamette Unit, west of Eugene, so I asked her for permission to hunt on their place. She asked her husband, Ron, also a student and my friend, who consented.

The Gibsons' property (otherwise known as "Fir Song Acres") would prove to be my "ace in the hole" that year and a couple others. Most of Gibsons' 130 plus acres was populated with second growth fir, though some small sections had been logged and replanted in recent years.

The next morning, Thanksgiving day, my twin brother, Rob, and I drove out to Fir Song Acres, having agreed to split the meat on any deer we killed that day. Considering Rob had only hunted one or two times all year, he stood to get a good deal if I bagged a deer.

It had frosted that night, and as Rob and I split up at daylight to work our first area, the brittle leaves from maple, oak and alder trees crunched loudly under our feet. By 8:45 we had worked a couple small areas and jumped two deer without getting a look. Temperatures had warmed considerably, thawing the leaves and brush which, of course, made for much quieter going. It was damp out and overcast. As in the past when hunting together, Rob and I maintained contact by whistling at regular intervals. I enjoyed hunting with Rob, probably because there weren't many things that we did together and working together on a common goal, that of trying to get a deer, was gratifying.

When we reached the top of the mountain across to the west from Gibsons' house, we split up again to work south along the east side of the mountain which was dominated by large Douglas fir with some oak and maple mixed in. Rob hunted below me on my left. A few minutes later, I tried to whistle Rob to my position to hunt what I felt looked to be a good area right of me to the west, but he didn't answer my whistles. He later said he had gotten fed up with my whistling and decided to ignore me while continuing the course we had begun. Since then, I too have become somewhat uncomfortable with whistling back and forth because I think the astute old bucks may sense something isn't right when they hear it.

Since Rob hadn't returned a whistle, I knew I better continue in the direction we were headed. I didn't know how far ahead of me Rob was, though I knew he would be below me a fair distance. Because I normally move at a snail's pace when I hunt, everyone, including Rob, gets impatient with me to some degree. That's another good reason why I like to hunt alone; I don't feel pressured to move faster than I'm comfortable with. In no way do I want to make it sound like I think my way is the best, or that it's even better than someone else's way of moving. Indeed, I believe that one thing that makes hunting so enjoyable to so many people is that each person can approach it his own way, unlike most jobs that require various tasks to be completed in a specific manner and within a certain time frame.

About a half-hour after continuing the hunt, I heard a gun-blast below me, but quite some distance ahead. Hoping Rob was the shooter, I worked over toward the edge of the bench I was on and in the direction of the shot, wanting to get myself into the best position for viewing the largest area in order to possibly intercept any deer running away from danger below. Less than two minutes later, I saw a flash out of the corner of my right eye and for some reason thought, "A bobcat." When I turned my head slowly, I saw it was a deer, so I released my safety. Then when the deer crested the ridge and turned toward me at thirty-five yards, I saw it had antlers. Honestly, that buck had a look on its face as if to say, "I sure got the best of that dumb hunter!" Unfortunately for him, he hadn't counted on me being there. Before he could notice me, I aimed for his chest between his front legs, and fired. Instantly, he bolted at full speed, but I managed to get off two more shots between trees. After my third shot, the buck jumped over a high log, and I saw his right front leg flop sideways telling me I had connected. Not seeing the deer after he cleared the log, I ran up and found him dead in the tall green ferns behind the log. He had run seventy-five yards from where I first shot at him. It turned out my first shot had blown his heart apart and, luckily, I had missed on the two running shots.

Rob called from way below, "Did you get him?"

I answered, "Yeh, it's a three-point!" A young, previously healthy three-point. Certainly, we had something to be thankful for on that Thanksgiving day!

Rob hustled up, arriving a few minutes later, and shook my hand as he congratulated me. He told me he had jumped the buck and managed a quick shot with Dad's twelve gauge shotgun loaded with 00 buckshot. Apparently he had missed, and I happened to be in the right place at the right time to score. I believe wholeheartedly that our hunting strategy of one partner being low and one high while we worked sidehill, plus my reaction after hearing Rob's shot, were responsible for our success.

After tagging and dressing out the buck, we switched off packing it out to Rob's car. In those days I just tied the four legs together and hung them over my head and shoulder with the body hanging by my side for packing. However, the next season, a friend, Larry Ekberg, showed me the best way I know of for packing out a deer, that of making the deer into a "backpack." (The deer backpack is explained in a separate chapter.)

Besides showing me the backpack method of packing deer out, Larry also demonstrated his way of field-dressing deer, and he sold me on that, too. I'm not going to explain it, however, because I'm sure that most hunters already have a technique that works well for them. I will say, though, that the thing I especially like about Larry's field-dressing method is that the heart and liver are left attached inside the deer's body cavity, which means I don't have to hassle with those organs until I get the deer home.

While butchering the three-point buck a few days later I found a .22 caliber slug in the upper part of its neck, just a millimeter shy of the spine. The wound was nicely healed over. Truly, this buck had lived a charmed life until he met up with the red-headed twins from Dexter.

*Blessed on Thanksgiving Day.*

# FALL 1983
# A BIG ONE FALLS

I missed the opportunity to hunt on opening morning because my work schedule at States Industries had me doing clean-up Fridays to Sundays. I did, however, get out at first light on the following Monday, though nothing noteworthy occurred. Having Mondays through Thursdays off allowed me to hunt a lot that year, and I saw numerous deer.

On October l8th, a warm dry day, my new friend Wayne Dale and I went hunting together on the north side of Lookout Point Reservoir. Wayne and I hit it off well right from the start, as he was a barrel of laughs.

The first day that Wayne and I hunted together, he looked at my rifle and asked, "Why doesn't your rifle have a sling?"

I responded, "It did, but it was just one more thing that could make noise, so I took it off." (Incidentally, I don't hunt with my sling on my weapon for two reasons: it can make noise, and it creates extra movement. I do, however, carry it with me sometimes.)

By lunch on the 18th, Wayne and I had hunted a couple areas without seeing any deer. After lunch we split up to hunt some second growth fir off Wimble Pass Road, about four and a half miles above Lowell. Wayne went low while I went above him. After about half an hour, I came to an area with a mossy forest floor decorated sparingly with ferns and having good visibility, and I thought, "Alright!, this is the kind of area I've been looking for."

Just then, Wayne came walking up out of the trees below me and said, "I'm gonna go on up the hill and hunt that timber above you."

"Okay," I replied, "I'm gonna go ahead and continue out this way," not giving Wayne any hint of my renewed optimism.

As we parted company, I proceeded into the area ahead of me to the west. About twenty minutes later, at 12:30, as I was making a detailed sweep with my binoculars, I spotted a buck feeding in the timber to my left. He hadn't noticed me even though I was only forty-five yards away. He was eating ferns, raising and lowering his antlers as though they were tree branches. I readied for a shot but didn't have a good opportunity because only the buck's head and the rear two-thirds of his body were visible. Since the tree that blocked my view of the buck's vitals was quite close to him, moving a few feet would not have helped much. I could have waited for him to move into the clear, but I wasn't sure whether he would sense my presence or not. I did know, however, that the wind blowing out of the west was in my favor. Opting not to wait for a better shot, I aimed just behind the tree into his liver area and fired. Instantly, he dropped to his knees. As I advanced on him, I yelled several times for Wayne. When he finally acknowledged, I hollered, "I got a buck!" As soon as the buck saw me, he jumped to his feet and began slowly trotting off, though he was obviously very sick. I aimed at his neck, but found my gun had jammed. (Later I discovered that the top of the magazine had gotten bent in slightly, interfering with the shell's loading.) Trailing the slow-moving buck, I managed to free the shell and chambered it. I then took a quick shot at the buck's neck at thirty feet but somehow missed. Taking more careful aim, I dropped him with my next shot. My first shot had torn through his liver, a fatal wound. The big buck was a beauty, sporting a very nice, high, symetrical three by three rack—though lacking eye guards—with a 14 1/2-inch inside spread.

Wayne arrived momentarily and congratulated me as he inspected and admired my big buck. At that time, Wayne had not yet killed his first buck though he scored on a nice three-point a couple years later.

To a hunter who has never killed a blacktail buck or perhaps never seen one while hunting, getting one can seem like an unobtainable feat. I know because I used to think so myself. Since success is built upon success, the inexperienced hunter must somehow persevere long enough to taste that first triumph; then I guarantee that if he is truly cut out to be a hunting addict, he will be hooked for life. I suggest that the novice hunter get out with a more experienced one whenever he has the opportunity. Not only will he appreciate the company, he can learn some of the do's and don't's of pursuing blacktails. Another thing he or she can do to stave off the discouragement that can come with not bagging one's first deer after many hours of hunting is to set other goals for why he or she is in the woods during all kinds of weather. I've discovered that just being in the wild, observing and learning about all of the animal and plant life, is very gratifying in and of itself. One will be amazed at how many sounds he will hear, fragrances he will smell, and activity he will see once he becomes attuned to the forest environment.

Another very important factor in maintaining a positive outlook while afield is to dress warmly enough to stay comfortable. Nothing can ruin a hunter's day like getting drenched and becoming very cold. I've had numerous miserable experiences while hunting because I was insufficiently dressed for the weather conditions. For example, one time I was hunting the north side of Lookout Point, high above the lake and about a mile from my car. A strong wind came up, blowing in a bad storm from the northwest. I was dressed in only bluejeans, a long-sleeve shirt over a short-sleeved one, and my ball cap and leather boots. In no more than half an hour the weather changed from being a dry and balmy sixty-five degrees to downpouring and forty-five degrees. At first I thought I would wait out the storm under the canopy of a large cedar tree, but then foolishly got impatient to continue hunting. I left the comfort of the cedar tree and slowly worked my way back toward the car. Immediately I was soaked to the bone from head to toe, and it wasn't long before I began shaking persistently. If I had seen a deer, I could never have held steady enough to shoot it. Continuing to fight my way through scotch broom, blackberries and salal, I finally reached my vehicle. It took me several minutes to work my keys out of my soaked, sleek jeans because my fingers were immobile and throbbing. Fortunately—as is always the case when I'm hunting or trapping—I had a complete change of dry clothes in my vehicle to put on, and in minutes I was beginning to thaw out. Believe me, I've

Buck taken in mid day (1983)

been in a lot worse predicaments, but this one could easily have been avoided with a little fore-sight and better judgment. We hunters are sometimes amused when we hear such tales of another hunter's stupidity, but we can all testify that at the time the situation is anything but funny. In fact, over the years many hunters and outdoorsmen have lost a few fingers or toes, or their lives, because of poor fore-sight or bad judgment in the face of inclement weather. As the above experience demonstrates, it doesn't take extremely cold weather and snowy conditions for a hunter to be in danger of hypothermia. As a matter of fact, most outdoorsmen go afield much better prepared when the weather is very cold than when it is relatively mild, though wet.

Incidentally, when I went along on a hunt with Wayne a day or two after getting my big buck, I observed that his gun was missing the sling it had earlier, and I asked, "By the way Wayne, what happened to your sling?" Instead of answering, he just got one of his typical big grins, half hidden by his black mustache, and we both had a good laugh. Wayne sure is a great-natured guy whom I definitely enjoyed being with. As I've gotten older, I've become more appreciative of the satisfying friendships I've had with people like Wayne.

Another person that I hunted with several times during the 1983 and 1984 seasons was my Uncle Ed Vohs. I really enjoyed his company too as I looked up to him a great deal. He was retired from the Air Force and Postal Service. He and I joked a lot throughout the day between hunts, and he treated me very well, as though I were his own son. Because he was a good whistler and I never have been, he poked fun at me in that respect at opportune moments. Sometimes when we would be whistling back and forth to maintain contact in the brush, I'd be doing a very mediocre job of it, and knowing that Uncle Ed was chuckling to himself about my pathetic whistling, I'd get to laughing—quietly, of course—and then my attempts to whistle became totally fruitless. Finally, Unck had put up with enough of my incompetence and handed me an empty shell casing, imploring me, "Here, why don't you use this to whistle with." Needless to say, we both had a good chuckle, but the shell did solve my puckering problems.

One time during the 1983 hunting season, Uncle Ed and I were hunting the north side of Lookout Point Reservoir and were maintaining contact by whistling, when a very long train passed by on the opposite side of the lake. When the train was finally well past, and the woods had returned to a quiet state, I whistled for Uncle Ed but got no return whistle. I whistled several more times, increasing my volume with each effort. After a few more minutes and no reply to my whistling, I worked around the ridge toward the south where I had last heard him tootle, but couldn't find him. Still I got no response to my whistling, so I became a little anxious. Hoping and figuring that he may have gone down the canyon on the south side of the mountain, I turned back to the west deciding to continue working the southwest slope as we had planned. I was quite familiar with the whole area we were hunting, but Uncle Ed wasn't. We both routinely carried compasses, but on that day they weren't important because it was clear and sunny out.

We had parked Uncle Ed's car down on the main North Shore Road near mile-post ten and had driven my car up to the top of School Creek Road with the idea of hunting back down to his car, a pretty fair distance below.

Since Uncle Ed was fifty-nine and carrying some extra weight—though he was on a daily walking routine and in decent shape—I became more and more concerned that maybe he had suffered a heart attack. My mind was no longer totally on hunting. About forty minutes later, I reached the North Shore Road and walked the short distance to Uncle Ed's car. When he didn't show up after awhile, I really started to worry about him and called his name toward the mountain numerous times. Still there was no answer. I certainly did not like the prospect of hiking back up the mountain through some dense brush to look for him, especially, knowing that if I found him, he would most likely be dead. I kicked myself for not searching for him on the mountain until I found him. After waiting at the car for another forty minutes, a pickup came down the road from the east, and who but Uncle Ed was sitting in the back. I was one very relieved nephew! He jumped out of the back holding his rifle and not containing the huge grin on his face, while he explained to me that when he had lost contact with me, he had continued on around the mountain to the south and worked his way down to the road. But unknowingly, he had walked away from where his car was parked. The lesson I learned was that when hunting with any person whose health I have any question about, I must maintain or regain contact with him before proceeding with my hunt. With a younger person I wouldn't have worried at all about the possibility of a heart attack.

For the mushroom connoisseurs, I'll mention that while hunting the same area another day that season, I found a much-coveted cauliflower mushroom that weighed in at over five pounds and provided me with a unique culinary treat. Since then I've found half a dozen more of those rare giant-sized mushrooms, all growing at the base of old-growth fir or cedar trees.

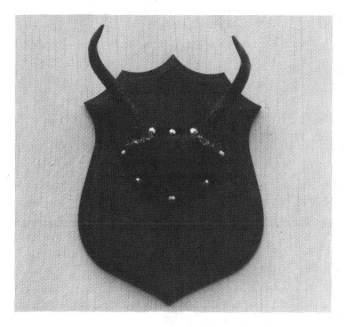

*A pretty spike.*

# FALL 1984
# CLOSE ENCOUNTER

Opening morning, on a dry temperate day, my brother Rob and I hooked up to hunt the north side of Lookout Point Reservoir. Unfortunately, my first two location choices were already accounted for by other hunters. My first choice was the burned hill at mile-post eleven, while my second pick was the huge clearcut across from the gravel pit at mile-post seven. Understandably, we were both disappointed because I hadn't considered a third option, and dawn wasn't waiting much longer. Rob had not hunted the north side before, whereas I had hunted and was familiar with much of it. Driving back down toward Wimble Pass Road, where I had connected on the big three-point the year before, Rob declared, "There's a road; let's take it!" I had hunted up there earlier and knew there was a nice clearcut adjoined by large firs, but I just hadn't thought of that spot. On one of my previous hunts in the timber above the unit, I found two four-point antlers on the same deer trail not fifty feet apart. They were not from the same deer, however, as they had come off the same side.

Anyway, I agreed with Rob to hunt that area, and when we drove in we found no one there ahead of us. I felt our chances were good. Of course, when it comes to outdoors, Rob is the eternal optimist, so expecting success was nothing unusual for him. Though he isn't possessed by the drive to hunt, fish, and trap like I am, he certainly has a knack for being in the right place at the right time when he is afield. Sometimes I think I must be an idiot, considering how many hours I had to devote to the outdoor sports before I became moderately successful. I think Rob is probably more of a natural outdoorsman than I am.

After parking the car some distance from the clearcut, we walked the skid road a short distance together until it split. I had explained the lay of things to Rob, so he took the road going up hill to the northwest and to my right, while I stayed in the bottom heading west. The wind was out of the north. I hadn't gone thirty feet, when two deer jumped out of the brush onto the skid road about twenty-five yards ahead of me. However, it wasn't quite light enough to immediately determine if they had antlers or not. Standing motionless with my scope trained on them, I watched as they milled around, facing away from me. I'm sure they had winded Rob and that's why they had jumped out of the blackberries and scotchbroom in the first place. Within two minutes, I identified both deer as does. So when they went around the corner of the road, I quietly hustled back to the fork and signaled to Rob that we had action, to be ready. I then continued on down the road behind the deer. I kept track of the two deers' progress as they moseyed along on the dirt road for over 200 yards, while moving along myself and glassing the young reprod unit to my north as the day dawned. That unit had uneven terrain, like most of the Cascade Mountain's foothills, so Rob and I were going to work it out as appropriate later on.

About twenty-five minutes after daylight, I heard, "Boom, boom," followed three seconds later by "boom, boom," from Rob's direction. Instinctively, I ducked down at the sound of his first two shots and then quickly moved into position for optimum viewing. Immediately, a spike jumped toward me out of some thick brush between Rob and me. He was nervously looking back as if waiting for another deer. A couple seconds later, a wide-racked buck jumped out also, just as I had hoped. When the big buck turned sideways to me at a distance of fifty yards, all I saw on his left antler was a wide fork. At that instant, I couldn't tell if he had any more points or not. At once, both bucks, oblivious to my presence, kicked it into bouncing mode, going broadside to me for a short distance and then turning away to the north, making any shot attempts futile. As they bounded away, I could see both deer most of the time through my scope, though they were partially obscured by the surrounding vegetation. I took my first shot at the big buck as the deer were bouncing seventy-five yards out, but they kept going. They continued bouncing until they were over 100 yards away. Finally, when they were a good 150 yards distant and quite aways up the hill from me, they turned to the left and slowed to a trot and then a fast walk. The spike was still in the lead as I got off two more off-hand shots on the big buck, which presented a broadside profile. Then both deer disappeared from sight. A minute later I saw the spike go up, and then over the next ridge, but I didn't see the big buck again.

Rob yelled, "Did you get him?"

"I don't know," I answered, "He was still on his feet after my third shot! Did you get one?"

He hollered, "Yeh, I got a three-point!"

"Good going!," I said, "I'm gonna go see if I can find mine."

I was happy for Rob—it was his first deer—but worried about whether I got mine.

Hurrying up to where I had last seen the buck, I looked for him and blood, but found neither in a brief search. Then I went down to where Rob was, anxious to see his prize, and I congratulated him with a handshake and a slap on the back. We were both pumped!

He exclaimed, "I spotted two deer standing by some blackberries about fifty yards away from me; one of them was partly behind a tree and I couldn't tell what it was. But I immediately saw the one was a legal buck and shot it just behind the left shoulder as it stood angled away from me. Since it didn't go down, I shot again until it finally did. At the sound of my first shot, the other deer and one more took off running. I saw the antlers on the big one and thought about shooting it. But you had told me not to shoot a deer for you, so I didn't." I then told him how I had responded when I heard his shots.

After Rob gutted his three-point—which he had hit twice in the ribs, destroying the lungs, and once in a flank—we hid it, and then went to do a thorough search for my buck. After ten minutes of looking, I found a spot of blood three inches in diameter where he had obviously stood momentarily. I got excited, knowing we both had our bucks opening morning. However, Rob cautioned me not to get too ecstatic until we found the buck. We began finding tiny spots of blood on the ground, and some rubbed on grass, at wide intervals going up hill along the draw. I was sure we would find him somewhere there in the clearcut. But finally, after tracking a very faint blood trail

200 yards up into the timber, we lost all sign. We searched for almost two more hours without any luck. I was sick about it.

Later, around noon, after we had gotten Rob's deer out and phctographed, I called a houndsman I knew and asked if he would track the deer with a couple of his dogs. Unfortunately, he declined for several reasons. After that I returned alone to the area where I lost the buck and looked for a long time more. Regrettably, I did not find the wounded deer. I was remorseful enough about it that I said I wasn't going to hunt anymore. By the next day, though, my innate love for deer hunting had caused me to change my mind.

I now believe, after many more years and kills, that the big buck I lost was likely only superficially wounded, probably on the underside of his body. I've observed the way many deer react and bleed when hit in the vitals or gutshot, and the buck I lost didn't fit into any of those scenarios. Unfortunately, superficial wounds are also sometimes deadly on big game. They just take longer to kill. I can only hope that the big buck survived.

As evidence of how intense and traumatic the search was for that deer and its blood, I dreamt about it several times after that. And even worse, every leaf or blade of grass I saw during the remainder of the season that had even the slightest shade of red, caused me to think I had found blood. This happened even when I was hunting completely different locations. I've told several other hunters this, and a couple of them reported experiencing similar thoughts and emotions upon seeing shades of red in the woods after intensely tracking a wounded animal's blood trail- regardless of whether they found the animal or not.

A couple of related experiences demonstrating how a human's senses are acutely tuned while hunting—at least for me—are how my senses of smell and hearing take me back to the woods long after the hunt is over. Often I will hear leaves rustling or the breeze blowing while lying silently in bed at night after a day of deer hunting despite the fact that neither leaves or the wind are audible from my bedroom. As to my sense of smell, I sometimes have vivid memories of prior deer kills

*Robin Murphey bags his first buck.*

come to mind at just the smell of gun-powder, or when I get wind of a deer while in the woods. For me the memories of earlier successful hunts are pleasant. In a way, these sensate experiences are similar to the way odors and sounds—such as hearing a particular song—can so easily take us back to moments long left in our past. Many military veterans experience some of the same emotions they experienced at certain moments during their past armed-service when just the right sound, sight, or smell occurs years later. For me, the smell of a diesel-engine running often takes me back to my submarine or the submarine base. I enjoy that because I have many fond memories of my years on the submarine.

Speaking of sounds, sights, and smells stirring up past feelings, there may be no animal that affects most humans' emotions as negatively as snakes do. Out here on the west coast of the United States, outdoorsmen have only one poisonous snake specie which they need to be alert for: the rattlesnake.

Here in Western Oregon, a hunter does not generally have to be concerned about having an encounter with a rattlesnake. I've seen only one live one while hunting, and it was a baby about ten inches long, sporting one rattle. I spotted it on a dry rocky knoll near Riddle, Oregon, in Douglas County. It was the only time I hunted that area, though not because I saw the snake. However, whenever I hunt or hike the rockier areas in the mountains of Lane County, I keep an eye out, just in case.

Curt Hensley, now deceased, of Lowell, once told me that years ago he and several other local men used to go up in the mountains just east of Lowell and hunt rattlers in the rocky areas when the snakes would first begin leaving their dens in the springtime. He said he and the other men killed hundreds of rattlers. Because the rattlers would den in the same places each year, he said that finding them was easy. Eventually, he said, they became scarce. Just recently when I talked to Curt's wife, Ruby, who still lives in the Lowell area, about the rattlesnakes, she told me that when her and Curt moved to Lowell in 1947 and for years after, they found and killed rattlers on their place regularly throughout the summer. Sometimes the snakes would even be right outside the doors of their house. She said they killed one on their place that had thirteen rattles. Over the years, however, the rattlesnakes were seen less and less until finally they weren't observed at all. Ruby said, "It's been over ten years since we saw a rattler on our place." One could only speculate on the reasons for the few sightings of recent years. Certainly the killing of rattlers at their dens in the spring and the influx of people with the resultant logging and land clearing (especially the building of Lookout Point and Fall Creek Reservoirs) along with the increased activity could all be factors. Of course, since rattlesnakes are predominantly nocturnal in their activities, an accurate assessment of their presence may not be possible in many areas.

Although rattlesnakes are not of much concern to blacktail hunters here in the Northwest, I've found that yellowjackets and hornets certainly can be. It seems that hornets, and especially yellowjackets, love to build their nests in the ground right next to deer trails. At least that's where I run into them, since I'm always walking on deer trails. Actually, I almost always detect the nests before it's too late and make a minor detour in order to avoid them. As 1984 was a tough-luck year on deer for me, it also proved to be a bad one for yellowjacket encounters. Twice during the fall hunt I failed to notice a ground nest before being stung. One morning, while still-hunting down a ridge above the rock cliffs on Lookout Point Reservoir's north side, the first indication of trouble came when I got stung in the back of the neck. Immediately, I took off running as I looked back at the swarming bees from the nest I had just walked over. I got stung again on my chest and managed to swat off a couple other yellowjackets that were attempting to crawl under my outer shirt. Luckily, the two stings were the extent of the damage inflicted. One other day, earlier in the season, I stirred up a

different nest, but was able to escape with only one sting. Since I swell up pretty badly from yellowjacket stings, I really cringed when I thought of how much worse I could have been stung in both cases.

Besides ground nests, the large bald hornets seem to favor madrone trees in or near clearcuts for nesting sights. A typical hornets' nest will be ten to eighteen inches around and gray. Sometimes I'll sit down and watch the activity at a tree nest for several minutes through the safety of my binoculars.

As everyone knows, black bears like honey. The fact is, black bears like eating bees, including hornets, and bee larvae, too. And as they are opportunistic feeders, they will readily dig up any nests they happen upon in their travels, since they are basically impervious to bee attacks. I find dug-up nests every year.

Though I saw at least two three-points or better during the regular season, besides the opening morning bucks mentioned earlier, I failed to get off a shot. I ended up going out to Gibson's woodlot in the Willamette Unit in November.

The morning of November 14th found me hunting in the young firs to the southeast below Gibson's house. Most of the trees were about twelve years old and were spaced at good intervals for maximum growth. I could see under many of them by crouching down. There were also a number of older second-growth firs and patches of very young firs. The ground cover in some places consisted of either blackberries, ferns, tall grass, dense scotchbroom, or a combination of some of these. The bulk of the forest floor, however, was covered with moss. The wind was gentle out of the northwest as I moved to the east.

At just after eight, the sun had broken over some of the treetops to the east enough to warm things and cause some shade problems. As I inched my way silently along on the mossy floor, looking and listening in the shade of some young fir trees, I spotted a large-bodied deer standing motionless, facing me at an angle behind some meagerly dressed young firs no more than twenty-five feet away. Though his head was not facing directly toward me, he seemed to be looking at me. However, since he was in the sunlight and I was in the shade, I don't know how well, or even if, he could see me. The branches near his head prevented me from clearly distinguishing his antlers, but there was absolutely no doubt in my mind that he was a real nice buck because his neck was huge and his body was much larger than any blacktail doe's. I can't accurately describe what went through my mind as far as my hoping he would hold still long enough for me to shoot him. As the buck stood there, I gently eased my safety off, raised my rifle slowly to my shoulder, aimed at his left shoulder, and fired. He stumbled noticeably and then was gone. Due to my opening day's traumatic experience, I was immediately worried when he was not lying dead where he had staggered. I marked a large fir tree nearby for reference and began looking around for sign, ending up at the muddy skid road fifty yards away where I scanned in both directions for the buck's tracks. Finding none, I determined he hadn't crossed it. Because the brush around the area was pretty thick, I became concerned about just where he had gone. Of course, I knew my shot had inflicted a fatal wound, so I would not have given up until I found him. Searching back closer to where he had stood, I got wind of him. All deer have a distinct odor, which I've often smelled while hunting, but this old buck had an exceptionally strong smell. Following the odor for about twenty-five yards, I found the deer leaning dead against a tree only twenty yards from where I had shot him. He was beautiful, sporting a heavy-based but tight three by three rack with eye guards. His lower back legs were stained a dark reddish brown because he had been urinating on his tarsal scent glands, located on the inside of the back legs; he was well into the rut. Upon field dressing him, I found that my 180 grain core-lokt bullet had devastated both of his lungs but had not exited, stopping underneath the skin behind his right shoulder.

As I finished gutting him, a neighbor of Gibsons' came hiking through the brush with his rifle in hand to where I was. He introduced himself, and looking with obvious envy at my buck, said, "I heard your shot, and wanted to see what it was about. I've been tracking this buck for the last three weeks. He sure is a beauty!" He then offered to help drag the animal out the two hundred yards to near Gibson's gravel road. Of course, I accepted the help.

Several of the deer I've killed over the years—to the present (December 1993)—have been testimony to my perseverance as a hunter. But no deer has proven my stealth like that big old three-point. That deer will always have a special place in my mind's trophy case, not only because of the intimate distance at which I killed him, but because he brought to a close the traumatic chapter that began on opening morning—wounding and not finding the big buck while hunting with Rob.

I want to make a comment regarding what Gibson's neighbor said about having tracked the big buck I killed for the previous three weeks. I think checking tracks is certainly useful in hunting blacktails. But due to ground cover and soil conditions, along with other deer traffic, I don't believe that following a single buck's tracks to a terminal point, that is, so as to get a shot at him, is very probable. Instead, a hunter should use the information gleaned from studying tracks to figure out travel patterns and then intercept an unsuspecting buck when he is in his tracks.

A beauty taken at close range.

# FALL 1985
# LATE SEASON LUCK

On Saturday morning, August 31st, the morning of my wedding day, I went out with my best friend, Jesse Chapman, a successful hunter--especially with coastal Roosevelt elk—to do some deer scouting up Getting's Creek fourteen miles southeast of Eugene. We saw over a dozen deer, including several bucks. In glassing one particular unit, we saw three different bucks, one of which was big and had a multi-pointed set of velvet-covered antlers. We also observed a few does in the unit. As it happened, there were a number of archery hunters in the area. We ran into one of them whom I knew as he was getting into his vehicle to call it quits for the day. Jesse and I were amazed that any hunter would stop hunting when there were so many blacktails feeding in sight, down in an accessible reprod unit. Undoubtedly, there were some deer we could not see also. I've never seen that many blacktails in the open during rifle season.

On the opening morning of rifle season, September 28th, my brother Rob and I hunted the same unit where Jesse and I had seen so many deer during the early archery hunt, but we didn't see a single live deer. Unfortunately, I did find a dead forked-horn which was still in full velvet in that unit in the evening. (It looked like the same one I had spotted alive about thirty yards away when I was down in the unit scouting one evening three weeks earlier.) I also found a dead doe in a nearby unit earlier in the day. Neither had arrows in them, and both had obviously been spotlighted less than three weeks earlier from the road above the respective units . That sort of unjustifiable slaughter gives hunters a bad reputation, despite the fact that poachers and spotlighters are not hunters by any stretch of the term.

1985 was the first year in which I drew a doe/spike permit for the Dorena Unit, which makes up the northwest portion of the larger Indigo Unit southeast of Eugene. The permit allowed me to take a second deer in addition to the one my general buck tag was good for. Shortly before dark on October l7th, a warm, dry day, my new friend and hunting partner, Jim Dormer, and I were riding in his Ford 4X4 pickup on a gravel road up Anthony Creek (a tributary of Lost Creek which empties into the Willamette River) on our way to our last stop. We came around a bend in the gravel road, and suddenly Jim announced, "There's your doe." We simultaneously saw four deer in the road about fifty yards ahead. As he stopped the truck, I jumped out and aimed, but forgot to chamber a round. (Nowadays I won't shoot an animal I spot from my vehicle, but at that time I would still consider doing so.) As I chambered a shell, the deer took off running down the road and then jumped into the brush on the left shoulder. I ran after them, heading into the timber where they had gone. It was late enough that it was darker in the trees than on the road, though I could still see well enough. Hiking slowly up the hill, I searched for the deer while Jim drove the truck on past me and around the next left-hand bend in the road and parked. After I had hiked fifty yards into the woods, where tall ferns abounded, a deer suddenly moved up the hill to my left about thirty yards away. As it climbed the hill going to my right, I took a well-aimed shot at the deer's right rib-cage from a rear quartered angle and instantly lost sight of it. (When my 30.06 recoils, it's not uncommon for me to lose sight of the animal as well as have my ears deafened for a second or two from the loud blast.) I searched the area for several minutes, sure I had connected, but could not find the deer. Darkness was beginning to close in fast, so I grew concerned.

Jim yelled from below, "Did you get it?"

I answered, "I was right on it when I pulled the trigger, but I can't find it."

"I heard something fall over to your right," Jim said.

Looking farther over toward where Jim had indicated, and down a steep bank, I found the deer lying at the bottom.

"I found it! It's a nice spike!" I exclaimed. "Why don't you bring the flashlight up with you, so I'll have a little more light to gut it out by."

As far as spikes go, it was a good one, with six-inch-high, curved antlers that looked pretty. Having Jim hear the young buck fall was a good break, certainly saving time in finding it. I've learned that a guy really needs to persist in looking for wounded game, believing that he hit it until evidence proves otherwise. In the thick brush of Western Oregon, I would be willing to bet that hundreds, if not thousands, of deer are wounded and lost each year. Many times a deer will show little if any sign of being hit and will get clear out of sight within seconds. Often there is not much blood to trail, though at times there is massive external bleeding. Tracks can be followed, but can be difficult to distinguish. Clipped hair can sometimes be found at the spot the deer stood when shot. (Clipped hair is much more prevalent when a deer is hit by an arrow than when hit by a bullet.) Freshly scuffed or turned soil, moss and leaves are a good clue to follow. Rain is the tracker's worst enemy because it washes away most of the sign. A mistake I've made consistently is to fail to back-track the deer I've killed to learn more about what sign to look for when in the future the need arises to track a wounded animal. Usually I'm in too big a hurry to get the deer home, especially if it's a nice buck. Two years ago I began carrying orange surveyor's ribbon when hunting to use as needed in tracking a wounded animal or to retrieve game, as in elk hunting.

Later in the season on the first morning of Hunter's Choice, a Saturday, Jim and I went hunting on the mountain behind Denny's Restaurant on Interstate Five just south of Eugene. I had had my sights on a nice spike for several minutes and had later jumped a large-antlered buck on that same hill two evenings before. About an hour after first light, as we were hunting the east side of the mountain and were about a hundred yards apart, I heard a single gunshot from behind me in Jim's general direction. Closing the distance some, I watched and listened for any deer movement. Less than a minute had passed, when somebody yelled excitedly. Wanting to see who it was and what the yelling was all about, I walked toward the source of the sound. When I got through the brush, I saw Jim standing near another young man who was bent down over a deer. Wasting no time, I hiked the remaining distance and saw that the guy had killed a small spike-buck which had three-inch-long antlers. The young man was ecstatic and proclaimed to Jim and me, "This is the third year in a row I've killed a spike on this hill on the opening morning of Hunter's Choice!" Honestly, he seemed as thrilled about that little spike as I had felt when I killed my first deer, a four-point. I remember thinking to myself at the time, "If I filled my buck tag with a puny deer like that three years in a row, I'd be disappointed rather than excited." Of course, I couldn't help but be happy for the guy because his enthusiasm was contagious.

Looking back, I have come to realize that the excitement exemplified by that young man over the harvesting of a mere yearling spike-buck epitomizes the spirit of the true hunter and sportsman. That is what hunting is all about—the euphoria of tasting success in the wild. Exactly what that success is cannot, and should not, be determined according to any one person's standards or even by comparing one season to another. In addition, a successful hunt should not be predicated simply on whether or not a kill was made, otherwise a hunter could only have a limited number of successful hunts each year. The hunt, in and of itself, should be rewarding to the hunter. If it's not, then maybe he needs to re-evaluate why he is afield in the first place.

On Monday two days after the young man killed his spike, Jim and I hunted the hill area northwest of and across 30th Avenue from Lane Community College. We had split up and had not been apart too long when I heard a shot from Jim's direction. About ten seconds later I heard another shot, usually a good indication of a kill, so I headed over to see. When I reached Jim, however, he was noticeably upset.

Standing over the doe he had just shot, he said, "I didn't kill her with my first shot. I broke her back."

I know from firsthand experience, that seeing a deer with a broken back is not a pleasant sight, as the deer drags its hind end around trying to get to its feet. I understood how Jim felt, and was moved by it. Jim is as tenderhearted a man as I've ever met.

I consoled him: "You know Jim, there are no guarantees that a hunter's first shot is always going to instantly kill the animal. You do the best you can to make a clean kill, but it's not always going to happen."

It is a rare hunter who has cleanly killed every animal he has ever shot at. We humans tend to naturally feel sorry for wounded animals, partly because we attribute human qualities to them. Specifically, we think of animals experiencing our same level of physical and emotional suffering. Certainly animals feel pain, but they don't understand pain's meaning. Like humans, they instinctively pull away from any source of pain. If they didn't, they wouldn't live long. However, animals do not regard pain in the same way humans do because they don't view their injuries as inconveniences or disabilities. When injured, they would not think, "I'm dying, who's going to take care of my children?" Or, "I'm too young to die; this hurts so bad." No, all an animal knows is that it is not able to get from point A to point B for some reason. When a trapped or wounded animal sees a trapper or a hunter approaching and tries furiously to get away or snarls and cries out, it is merely responding to its God-given survival instinct that compels it to fear and avoid other predatory animals. To deer and many other wild animals, man is a predatory animal.

Well, once again I ended up having to go back out to Gibsons' place in the Willamette Unit, as I failed to fill my buck tag during the regular season. On November 29th, the next to last day, there was a light snow on the ground when I began my hunt at dawn, though not much had penetrated the second-growth fir canopy where I was hunting. In the early afternoon I was slowly working along the same ridge where I had killed the three-point while hunting with Rob in 1982, when a deer suddenly startled and bolted from a small brushy bench below me to my left. I knew it was a buck at once even though I didn't get a good look at its head because it had a muscular body. However, I doubted that I would even get a shot at him since he disappeared behind some young maple and fir trees. When it seemed as if he had turned to his right, I readied myself in the only shooting lane I might get, a space about twenty feet wide between the big firs about 100 yards away on the flat sixty feet below me. There I held my scope, hoping he would cross. Sure enough, he appeared two seconds later, running away from me at nearly a broadside angle. When the front of his chest touched the center of my crosshairs, I squeezed, but he ran out of sight behind the firs to the right. I thought, "I doubt I hit him, the way he was running, but if I did, he'll be down there somewhere." Not fifteen seconds later, the deer came staggering back out into the shooting lane and dropped dead in the tall ferns. I immediately hurried down, anxious to see his rack. When I reached him, I saw he was a forked-horn with straight and tall antlers that looked like daggers, unique though not pretty. I figured him to be a two-and-a-half year old deer. Upon dressing him out, I found that my bullet had ruined his liver.

Interestingly, it has been my experience, both up through the killing of this dagger-horned fork and with every deer I have harvested since then, that any deer hit in the liver was neutralized almost immediately, displaying definite signs of being hurt. On the other hand, deer shot in the lungs or heart sometimes travelled as much as seventy-five yards before going down. Additionally, the deer that had no idea of my presence when shot consistently went down sooner than those that knew I was nearby.

I was thrilled to get the dagger-horned fork even though its rack was definitely inferior to the previous four year's bucks' racks. When I got home with him, I called Jim who then came over to see the deer.

*The Dagger-horned fork*

# DEER MEAT'S QUALITY

From my experience in eating deer meat over the years—and I have eaten meat from several dozen different deer, including many killed by friends—I have determined that there are several factors that influence the meat's toughness and in some cases its flavor. Those factors are (1) the amount of body fat on the deer, (2) the circumstances of the kill, (3) the animal's age, (4) the animal's sex, (5) the meat's aging time, and (6) the kill date.

First, the more fat on a deer when it is killed, the better. On the other hand, it is imperative that as much fat as possible be removed from the meat when it is butchered because of the tendency for wild-games' fat to go rancid while in storage. I always use beef fat in making venison burger. Second, when considering the circumstances of the kill and comparing the meat of several similar-age deer with comparable amounts of body fat, I found that deer killed after being startled had tougher meat than the ones that were not alarmed before being killed. The ideal situation is when a deer does not know the hunter is present and is killed instantly by the first shot. Third, younger animals typically are more tender than older ones. Fourth, as a rule does are more tender than bucks. However, a "wet-doe," one that has been nursing a fawn or two, and has no body fat can be relatively tough. Fifth, aging meat before butchering helps to tenderize it because the muscle tissue begins to break down (the first stage of rotting). I normally let my deer meat hang for three or four days in my shop where the temperature averages in the forties or low fifties by late October when I typically get my deer. I know some hunters that let their meat hang several days longer than that before tending to it, and I think their meat is even more tender than mine. I have found, though, that my meat lasts longer and holds its flavor better in the freezer if I don't let it age more than five or six days before cutting it. That's something to keep in mind. Actually, meat can be aged even after being cut-up, either before being frozen or after it is thawed out before cooking it. It's just easier to age the whole carcass in one step. The final factor, I feel, affecting meat quality is the date the kill is made, that is, the time of the season. Here I am mainly referring to whether the deer is killed before the rutting season (breeding season) or during it. Personally, I don't feel that the rut itself has that much bearing on the meat's quality. Some hunters see a big old buck with a swollen neck in the back of a truck and immediately comment on how tough the meat will be or how gamey it will taste. I have not necessarily found that to be the case. If anything causes the bucks' meat to be tougher during the rut, I believe it is their higher activity level combined with the lower percentage of body fat they have as a result of eating less and chasing does more. I imagine that their increased adrenalin levels could have some effect also. However, I've never noticed any decline in the meat's taste when the deer was killed late in the season.

Some hunters will undoubtedly disagree with my above list of influencing factors regarding the quality of deer meat, and that's alright because I'm basing my opinion on my own experience. But since I have never been known to deliberately step around a controversial topic, I'll now mention what I believe are a few needless steps that many hunters take after downing an animal because they believe not to do so will negatively affect the quality of the animal's meat.

First, some hunters are thoroughly convinced that a deer's throat must be cut immediately after the deer is dispatched in order to bleed the deer. This procedure is not necessary because any chest cavity hit by a high-powered bullet will have already bled sufficiently. Besides, when the animal is field dressed, it will bleed out nicely. Being a trapper, I have eaten meat from several species of fur bearers, and specifically I have eaten a lot of meat from beavers. In some cases the beavers had been dead for up to four days before I skinned and butchered them. Certainly, they had cooled quickly and been kept quite cool before skinning. However, I never bled them, yet their meat was every bit as flavorful and tender as those that I handled within hours of being trapped. The key was in getting the meat cooled, not in bleeding it. A further example is that one year I had the unusual opportunity to eat a number of steaks from a small-bodied deer that was not killed by a gunshot, nor had it bled at all, either externally or internally. It had been dead for over twenty-four hours and had cooled well by the time the meat was procured, yet its meat was tender and tasty.

While I'm on the topic of blood, I should say that I do take care to trim away bloodshot meat from the vicinity of any bullet wounds, putting all that is salvageable—that which hasn't been turned into mince meat—into a jerky brine to soak for a day or so before smoking it. The salt in the brine does a nice job of drawing the blood out of the meat.

A second unnecessary step that many hunters take is cutting away the tarsal scent glands, located on the inside of the back legs at the heel, because they firmly believe that leaving them in place could taint the deer's meat. However, I've eaten meat from deer that had these glands removed immediately after being killed, and it was no better than any of the meat from the many deer in which the glands were left attached.

Third, some hunters swear that a dead animal's hair must not come in contact with its raw meat, so they go to a lot of extra work to ensure that doesn't happen. A hunter friend of mine from Montana once told me that if even one hair from an antelope touches any of its raw meat, all of the meat will be tainted. That definitely is not true.

I suspect that many of the hunters who take the steps just discussed have never tried not doing so. I figure, why should I go to any extra work if the final product's quality turns out the same either way.

Another area of concern to many hunters is the possibility of parasites in deer meat. (I am not a medical authority, and therefore, what I say concerning parasites is only my opinion based on my own limited experience. This discussion is included for interest sake only.) A couple of hunters over the years have told me that they had killed deer that were full of worms. Still others believe that deer meat must be well-cooked, as pork or bear meat is, because of potential parasites. Regarding the parasites, I eat most of my deer steak cooked medium-rare, and I have never had any health problems as a result. Nor have I heard of anybody else having any health problems related to eating undercooked venison.

Concerning the worms, I recall an incident ten years ago when two of my friends shot a nubbin spike (a yearling buck with very short antlers—under an inch and a half long) while hunting together. Upon returning from their hunt they skinned the deer and then cut it in half, each taking an equal portion. The one friend had handled a number of deer over the years and knew how to care for the carcass, while the other friend had never handled a deer before. The first friend had no problems with his half of the deer which he said was very tender and tasty. My other friend and co-worker, on the other hand, told me at work several days after killing the young buck that his deer meat was full of worms and that he had thrown all of it away. Same deer, yet one half was fine while the other, reportedly, had worms. My guess is that the one friend at some point left his portion of the carcass exposed long enough for flies to get into it and lay their eggs which, of course, developed into maggots. Any deer that is taken needs to have its carcass wiped totally clean after being skinned and then hung inside a cloth deer bag to keep flies and other pests off it. The only time the bag can be left off a carcass is if the temperature is too cold for flies to be active. I suspect that many of the worms that hunters find in their meat are actually maggots resulting from opportunistic flies. Incidentally, maggots are edible so even if a person inadvertently ate some in a piece of meat, they wouldn't hurt him.

There are many other theories and myths floating around regarding the treatment and preservation of big-game meat, but I think I've covered the most prevalent ones, so I'll leave it at that. Every deer I've killed was plenty edible which causes me to be skeptical of the few people who told me they had killed stinky, old, rutting bucks whose meat was so strong tasting they were forced to throw all of it away. Even if meat is especially strong, there are many ways to prepare and cook it to neutralize the strong flavor.

Suffice it to say that a deer that is cleanly killed, field dressed promptly and properly, and then skinned and wiped out, and hung to cool within a reasonable period of time (the same day), and aged according to personal preference, will provide the hunter and his family with many tasty and rewarding meals.

# THE DEER BACKPACK

Many hunters drag their deer out of the woods to their vehicles or their hunting camps which works well enough if there are two or more people. I've tried dragging deer, and it worked alright on the small ones when I was on fairly level or downhill terrain where I didn't have to travel sidehill. But with the big blacktail bucks—I'm not talking about the much larger mule deer or whitetails—carrying them by the backpack method was easier. Maybe for short stocky guys, who don't have to bend as far, dragging isn't so laborious. But I'm six-foot one-inch, and weigh 190 plus pounds, and my back doesn't like bending down to pull an animal along on the ground. After learning the backpack method of transporting deer from the woods I'm convinced it is the easiest way for a solo hunter to get a whole, unskinned deer out.

To make the deer backpack (Illustrated), the successful hunter should follow this procedure.

1   Make about a four-inch vertical cut in the skin on the front of what is often called the front knees. These joints function as knees though they do not have a patella- or knee cap. Anatomically they are correctly termed "wrists."
2.  Then peel the skin loose from the joint going all the way around to the back, and cut the tendons.
3.  The legs then break easily by twisting them at a ninety degree angle at the joint. This leaves each foreleg dangling by the skin still attached to the upper leg.
4.  After breaking the front legs, the skin is left intact and peeled down the forelegs a couple more inches.
5.  Then a four-inch slit is cut in the back legs just above the heel, between the tendon and the bone.

6. Next, the front forelegs are poked, hooves first, all the way through the holes in the back legs from inside to out side. This will form a T-hook of the front forelegs and the skin, locking the front legs to the back legs.

7. For the hunter's safety, red or orange material should be tied over and around the deer's antlers and upper back, if a buck, or around its upper back, if a doe.

8. Finally, the hunter should get down next to the deer and slip his arms through the legs, roll over so the deer is on his back, and slowly raise to his feet. He can then easily carry his weapon in one of his free hands.

I understand that drag ropes are popular back East where snow covered ground and relatively flat terrain are fairly common. However, in the typical areas I hunt snow is uncommon and the terrain is rarely flat (one exception being in bottomland along rivers). Often I have to carry my deer side-hill and over downed logs, up and down ridges, across brushy springs and creeks and through short stretches of moderately heavy brush. Getting my deer up off the ground and on my back has proven to be the quickest way to get the animal back to my vehicle. Obviously, a hunter that is carrying a heavy animal must take more care in traversing any uneven or brush-littered ground so as to avoid spraining or breaking a knee or ankle.

Upon arriving at home or camp after packing a deer out it is a good idea for the hunter to do a thorough check of his body for any ticks which may have come from the deer's hide. Although I have never had a tick imbedded in my skin after packing a deer out, I have found a couple on my body. Any time a hunter or trapper is in prolonged contact with a game animal, he becomes a possible host to any of several types of bugs living on the animal- particularly fleas and ticks.

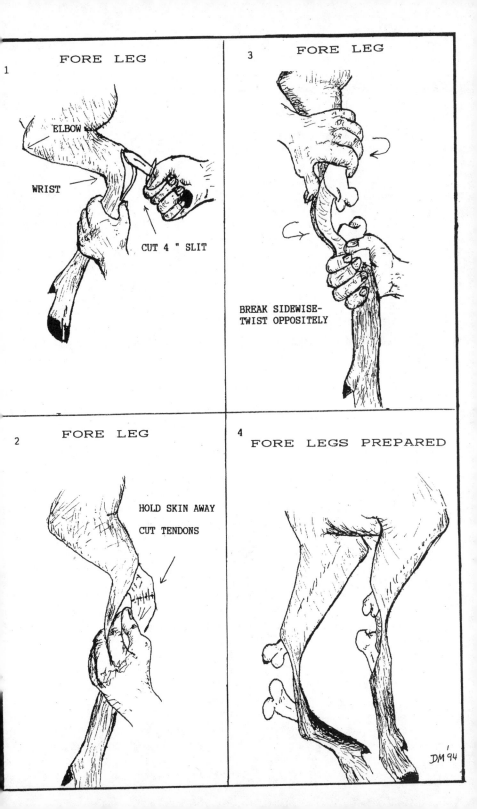

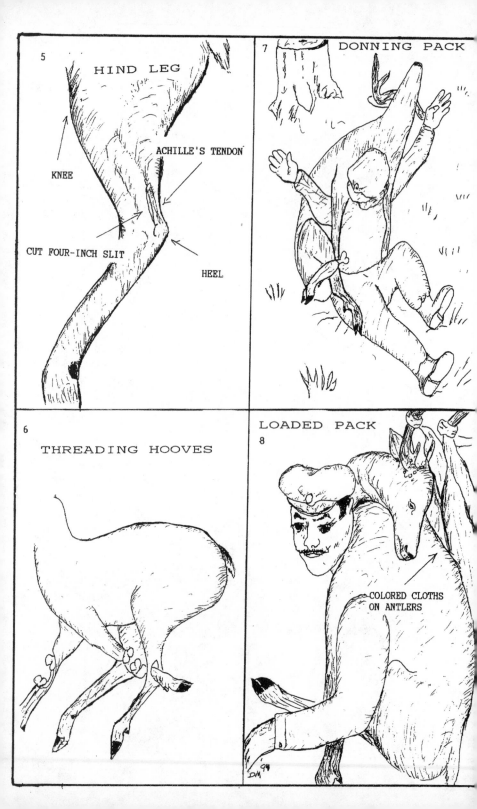

**5** HIND LEG

KNEE

ACHILLE'S TENDON

CUT FOUR-INCH SLIT

HEEL

**7** DONNING PACK

**6** THREADING HOOVES

**8** LOADED PACK

COLORED CLOTHS ON ANTLERS

# PARTNERS DIVIDING MEAT

After hearing a gunshot from over the ridge I was hunting along in pursuit of an elk, I decided to work over toward the shot in hopes of seeing a fleeing elk I could get my sights on. A minute later, when I was perhaps seventy yards away, I heard what sounded like two people arguing. Moving in closer and peering through the brush, I could see a man and a woman, both holding rifles, arguing as they stood over a large animal laying on the ground between them. The woman yelled, "It's my elk!"

"No it's not your elk!" shouted the man.

Pointing the muzzle of her rifle at the man, the lady shouted, "It is too my elk!"

Finally the man conceded, "Okay, Lady, you can have your elk, but would you please let me get my saddle off of it?"

Although this joke, which most of us have heard in one form or another at some time, depicts an extreme situation, the reality is that hunters, including partners, have been known to get into some downright serious altercations over who shot an animal or who gets to keep it. I've even heard of friendships ending over disagreements about the way a game animal's meat was divided. So how should hunting partners divide up their meat? I view elk and deer differently in this regard.

Because elk are harder to come by and they have so much meat, normally hunters hunt with the idea that any elk killed are party elk. By that I mean that each hunter present in the party takes home meat—normally a quarter. If it's just a two person party and they bag an elk, they split the meat equally. If three hunters are teamed up on a hunt, then often the one who shot the elk will take half, while the others take a quarter of the meat. Some other possible factors that may be considered when apportioning the meat are how much help the others gave in packing the meat out or whether one guy chased the elk out to a partner.

When I hunt deer with anyone, I try to make a point of addressing the meat issue prior to the hunt. If a person doesn't like my system he can choose to not hunt with me. I kill my buck regularly, and I count on getting my deer meat. I put in plenty of time in the bush hunting, and I also pass up some younger bucks while waiting for one I want. It wouldn't be equitable for me to split my deer's meat with someone who spends considerably less time hunting than I do but just happens to be with me when I get mine. After all, I'm done hunting at that point and can not ensure that my partner will come through with a deer of his own later to split with me. And what if he did kill one later, but had someone else with him who wanted half of its meat? There's not that much meat on a deer to begin with. The most I've ever gotten off a blacktail buck was a little over eighty pounds of boned out meat. Typically, a good-sized buck yields sixty to seventy-five pounds. Here is how I work the meat distribution: 1) If you kill a deer while hunting with me, I want no more than a pack of steak. 2) If I kill one while you're along, I give you two or three packs of meat—one of which is steak. 3) In addition, I am more than willing to go along with you, after I have already filled my tag, in order to run brush or do whatever I can to help you shoot your own deer. When Rob and I split the meat on the buck I killed in 1982, it was because we had agreed upon that before the hunt.

Each party of hunters, should decide before hunting exactly how any meat will be dispersed. Dividing up a game animal's meat is not an issue worth losing respect or a friend over. But that could certainly happen if things are assumed and not discussed between partners prior to the hunt.

# IS BEING QUIET IMPORTANT?

When I hunt, I try to be quiet. Believe me, I make some noise and even occasionally snap a limb. However, many hunters I've seen sound more like a cow tromping through the brush than a hunter who hopes to get a deer. Is being quiet really all that important? I believe most of the time it is. The hunter that can sneak very quietly through the woods, keeping the wind in his favor and not making any abrupt movements, has a good chance of seeing deer before they see him. Certainly a hunter on stand must be as quiet as possible in order to avoid alerting any approaching deer of his presence. Obviously, there are times when the ground cover—mainly consisting of leaves, twigs, and small branches—is so dry that it is impossible to move silently. Sometimes it's tough to even be quiet. Then the key is to move the way an animal would move. Animals often make noise when they move around in the woods. But their movement is irregular and the noise they make rustling leaves and brush, knocking fir cones out of trees, or snapping small limbs, is nothing like a hunter who moves along at an even pace, regularly popping limbs and even coughing and sneezing.

On the other hand, there are times when a hunter can use noise to his advantage. Sometimes, if he can see a lot of area in the woods or in a clearcut where there would be plenty of opportunity for a shot should he jump a deer, a hunter might want to deliberately tromp around in hopes of forcing a deer to move into the open. Hunters working as a team, such as in a drive, often intentionally make noise to try to get the deer moving. Usually does and younger bucks fall for this tactic easier than older bucks. Older bucks will typically either stay put while hunters pass close aboard, or they will sneak out ahead or behind the hunters without being noticed. Incidentally, at times a quiet hunter can use a noisier partner to his advantage, letting the noisier one push deer his way. This can be done while still-hunting (moving slowly along while hunting) or while doing a drive with one or more hunters on stand overlooking the probable escape trails that any deer would take in fleeing from a hunter or hunters moving through the brush where the deer are holding up.

*Who popped that limb? (ODFW Photo)*

# WHAT ABOUT
# HUMAN ODOR?

Most deer hunters agree that a hunter should always try to keep the wind blowing in his face or across his body when hunting deer so as to prevent deer ahead of the hunter or those in the direction he is facing if on stand from getting a whiff of his human scent. The reason for this, of course, is that deer fear men—as they fear other predators—and will instinctively avoid contact with them, immediately responding to any warnings their senses receive which betray a human's presence nearby. A deer's most reliable life-saving sense is its sense of smell. Deer pay great attention to the odors drifting in on the breeze, and nothing disturbs them more than getting a nose-full of human body odor or any of the other various odors that humans carry into the woods with them, via their clothes, footwear, hats, guns, and other hunting supplies. Think about it. If a deer <u>hears</u> a leaf crunch or a twig snap under a human foot, it is hearing a sound commonly made by many wild animals, particularly other deer. If a deer <u>sees</u> a hunter, it may not recognize him as a human. For example, when a hunter is motionless, a deer will often look right at him, stare for a prolonged period, and then go back to feeding or whatever it was doing, comfortable that it didn't see anything to be afraid of. However, if a deer <u>smells</u> the scent blowing right off of a hunter, it will instantly be alarmed. At the very least, the deer will turn its head and watch in the direction the foul smell came from. That already stacks the odds against the hunter's getting a shot. Often the deer will sneak out of the area ahead of the hunter's arrival, giving no clue of its presence. Many times the agitated deer will simply hide in thick brush, remain motionless, and watch the hunter pass by. At still other times a deer will noisily run off, perhaps stomping a foot first, or often it will blow a danger warning to other deer in the area.

Many expert deer hunters say it is extremely important that a deer hunter not touch any brush with his bare hands because to do so is to "scent-broadcast." By scent-broadcasting they mean that a hunter is spreading his human scent all over his hunting area, and that will have a detrimental affect on the deer activity in the area. These hunters also go to great length to hide or "eliminate" human odors associated with the clothing and footwear they use while hunting. Though I agree that re-peated human intrusion can definitely affect deer movement patterns, I do not agree that any human can possibly eliminate all of his human odors. All of our clothing and footwear has a human odor on it no matter what measures we take to prevent it. Besides that, we humans are constantly sweating even when we don't notice it, so our clothing, hats, and shoes will al-ways emit our odor to at least some degree. If a deer passes through the same spot where a man walked or rubbed up against any brush within the previous several hours, that deer will know a human was there before him. But how does the man's earlier presence affect the deer? In most cases, I think, it has little effect on a deer.

A coyote's sense of smell is about as impressive and dis-cerning as there is, and coyotes are generally very leery of hu-mans. Yet one professional Oregon state trapper I know of, who traps coyotes for damage control year-round and catches hundreds each year, sets his traps and makes his sets bare-handed. During his coyote trapping demonstration at the Ore-gon Fur Takers Rendezvous at Waldo Lake in 1992, this trap-per was asked why he doesn't wear gloves when trapping coyotes. He said, "It makes no difference to the coyotes, just to the trappers who believe they can't catch a coyote with a set made without wearing gloves."

A red fox is another fur-bearer considered to be extremely fearful of humans and their odor. In fact, for years I heard that only a good trapper using gloves when making his sets could catch fox. When I first began setting for fox, I took special care to keep my scent away from sets. I wore gloves to set traps and to make my sets. I even kept the fox traps and my gloves in sealed bags when they weren't in use. After a while I thought, "All these extra measures aren't worth the hassle."

Then I tried setting snares and leg-hold traps for fox bare-handed and found it made no difference in my catch. I still caught fox. Although I've done a limited amount of fox trapping, I am convinced that the secret to catching fox is in properly locating sets and in stabilizing traps so they don't move if an animal steps on the edges of them.

I figure that if coyotes and red foxes are not bothered all that much by a trapper's scent after he is long gone, then most deer probably don't get all that upset about a human's odor either when they encounter it several hours after a hunter was present. This is contrary to what many deer hunting experts would lead people to believe. One more example supporting my thinking on this is that on several occasions, when sleeping in my vehicle over-night during deer season, I looked out the windows during the night and saw deer—even bucks—feeding within ten yards of my vehicle, right where I had walked hours earlier.

Earlier I said that repeated human intrusion can affect deer activity. By that I meant that if a deer encounters a human more than once in the same area within a short time period—such as in consecutive days, or even several days apart—that deer generally will not frequent the same area again at the same time of day when the intrusion occurred for perhaps several days and in some cases for much longer. A big buck may go into extended hiding after only one encroachment. By "encounter," I am referring to a deer seeing, hearing, or smelling a hunter in the deer's immediate presence, not to a deer coming into an area hours after the hunter has left and smelling the hunter's odor on the ground or on brush. As I said earlier, I don't believe deer are influenced that much by residual human odor. The oldest bucks may be an exception. Because blacktails tend to be erratic in their feeding and activity patterns even when not disturbed, and because seeing the same deer in the same area at the same time of day on consecutive days is unusual, it's hard to say whether deer are absent from a particular feeding area as a result of recent human intrusion or for some other reason, such as the wind or weather.

I want to clarify that what I have discussed so far concerning human odor was done primarily in the context of still-hunting (my forte) or stalking deer. Since I have limited experience with stand-hunting, as of January 1994, I don't claim to be an authority on the effects of human scent on deer while on stand. However, I do understand the principle of "scent dispersal," meaning that the longer a hunter remains on stand at one spot, the more his scent gradually disperses and permeates the area around the stand. Obviously, this scent dispersement could alarm any deer wandering into the area. Can a hunter do anything to prevent the negative effects of his scent dispersing from his stand?

Previously I said that many hunters attempt to hide or eliminate their human odor. For example, some hunters make definite changes in their diets prior to and throughout a particular hunting season because they feel that their diet affects their body odor. Indeed, it is well known that one's diet can affect the potency of his or her body odor. I've found that some seasonings are especially offensive in their presentation in sweat, so much so that the effect is very noticeable to me. The way I figure it, if I can't tolerate my own odor, then certainly a big buck won't. Therefore, I try to avoid eating most seasonings just prior to and during deer season. (I didn't start this practice until a couple of years ago.) Besides not eating any seasonings during deer season, some hunters actually quit eating any meat during that same time frame because they believe that by doing so they eliminate their "meat-eater, predator" smell. They think that if they don't smell like a predator, then deer will not be as likely to react negatively upon getting wind of their odor. That all makes very good sense to me. Regardless, I like eating meat far too much to give it up in order to please the deer. (The deer would probably be much more pleased if all hunters gave up eating meat all year long. At least some of the deer would live longer, but then they would die a much slower death at nature's hands.)

Although I don't go to the lengths to eliminate my human odor that many hunters do, I agree that a hunter with less body odor will not be noticed as easily or at as great a distance by deer as one that "sweats like a hog." I don't think anyone would argue with that. Smokers are easier for a deer to smell than non-smokers. As a non-smoker, I can tell immediately upon meeting someone whether he or someone he has been around a lot smokes, just by the odor on his clothes. If it's *that* noticeable to me with my inferior sense of smell, then be assured, that odor doesn't escape a deer's notice either.

I could discuss many other factors that could influence a hunter's odor or measures that hunters take to fool a deer's olfactory, but I'll just mention two measures taken by some hunters. One is the practice by some hunters of taking baking-soda baths prior to and during the hunting season to eliminate body odor. The other is the custom of some hunters to put all of their hunting clothes in sealed plastic bags containing fir or pine sprays or whatever is a predominant plant in the area they hunt. These hunters believe that doing so will cover up and disguise

their scent. No doubt it helps. But as I said before, I don't believe it is possible to totally eliminate human odor. If I with my poor sense of smell (relative to most animals) can easily smell a deer when I'm down-wind from it, then I know a deer, whose very survival depends on it's excellent sense of smell, can smell me when I'm up-wind from it no matter what I do to eliminate my odor. The single most important measure a hunter can take to negate the effects of his scent on deer is to <u>keep the wind blowing in his face or across his body</u>. In other words, stay down-wind of the deer.

I've killed a number of old bucks, so I know it is possible to be successful on trophy-age animals without going to extreme lengths to disguise, cover up, or do away with human scent. I don't mean to downplay the value of taking various protective measures for containing human scent. It's just that I find all that extra effort more burdensome than beneficial. On the other hand, I can't argue with another hunter's philosophy or success record.

# ONE DEER
# HUNTER'S WOES

We have all known people who had a tremendous interest in and zeal for a sport or hobby in which they just were not meant to succeed. The old saying "If you can't play the game, then coach it or referee it" really applies to these people. I have a good friend who fits into this category when it comes to his pursuit of deer.

Mario Smith is six-feet-four, weighs 300plus pounds, has curly, short, dark hair and a mustache—he strongly resembles the star male character in the movie "Gator Bait," which was staged in the Louisiana bayous. Although he was born in Tacoma, Washington, Mario grew up in Louisiana and is most definitely a cajun at heart. I have never met another person that can tell jokes and keep an audience rolling with laughter the way Mario can. His repertoire of cajun and especially Boudreaux jokes is endless. Unfortunately, his efforts to bag a deer are anything but a laughing matter. I'll share a few examples of what I'm talking about.

Mario moved out to Oregon in the early '80's, which is when I met him. Several years earlier, he and a close friend were hunting white-tail deer in a Louisiana pine forest on the opening morning of deer season. (The first four days were reportedly Hunter's Choice.) About mid-morning, his friend happened upon a dead doe which had obviously been shot only a short-time earlier, since her blood had not yet coagulated. Looking around to ensure no one was watching, his friend pointed his rifle toward the sky and fired off a round. Immediately, he began hollering excitedly. Mario, only a short distance away, arrived post haste and was enlightened by his friend as to the details. When the two of them returned home later with the deer, they were queried immediately by their wives, "Did you guys shoot a deer?"

84

Being the good Christians that they were, the men didn't want to lie so they answered with the line they had already agreed upon. "God provided us with a deer."

When they then showed the whitetail doe to the women, they were again asked skeptically, "Did you guys really shoot this deer?"

Again Mario and his friend responded, "God provided us with this deer!"

Knowing better than to pursue the matter further, the women left it at that. As Mario's luck would have it, that doe was the closest he came to actually killing his own whitetail deer that year or in any others that followed in Louisiana.

In Oregon several years later, 1985, Mario actually killed his first deer. But he did it in a non-traditional way. For several weeks prior to deer season, Mario had arrived at church on Sunday mornings very much enthused about a big four-point blacktail buck he saw regularly in the mornings and evenings on his drive to and from home on a country road southwest of Eugene. He sometimes drooled as he went on and on about how he was going to get that four-point on opening morning. About two weeks before rifle season was to open, Mario arrived at church with an exceptionally downcast look on his face. Wondering what was wrong, I asked him. He related,

I was driving home from work [as a security guard] at three-thirty in the morning a few nights ago when a doe ran across the road about thirty yards ahead of me. I was only doing about thirty miles an hour and immediately thought, 'There's going to be a buck.' At that instant a buck jumped out of the ditch right in front of me, and I hit it with my right front fender. I got out of my car and found that I had killed it; apparently it's neck was broken. It was the same four-point I've been seeing every day.

Apparently Mario is a better shot with his car than he is with his rifle.

The next year, on the third Saturday morning of the 1986 blacktail hunting season, Mario awakened just after daylight and looked out the bedroom window of his house. Surprisingly, two young bucks were standing just outside his yard, munching on grass. He hurriedly grabbed his 30-30 Winchester, loaded it, and ran around the back of the house in order to sneak a shot at the larger of the two deer, a forked-horn. He stopped beside a tree no more than fifteen yards from the two deer and allegedly shot the larger one in the rib cage. Instantly, the young buck dropped to the ground, while the spike stood watching, not knowing whether to run away or wait for the forked horn. Mario, thrilled that at long last his moment of conquest had arrived and that he finally had bragging rights in the blacktail hunters' club, hustled toward the downed deer to administer the final dose. But when he opened the gate five yards from both deer, the forked-horn jumped to its feet, and the two bucks high-tailed it across the field away from Mario. Mario watched hopelessly as the deer proceeded to jump three fences and cross two roads before disappearing into the tree line nearly a mile away. At once, he looked the ground over where the buck had fallen and for some distance along the path the deer had exited on, but he found not a single drop of blood. Later, when he attempted to tell a group of his friends at Bible college that he had shot a buck, they merely responded, "No horns, no tales!"

*One of Mario's dreams (ODFW Photo)*

The following year on the fourth weekend of the general blacktail season—still never officially having killed a blacktail deer with a rifle—Mario took Todd, a friend and former Bible college classmate, with him to his hunting spot southwest of Eugene. Just after daybreak, Todd, who was using a borrowed gun, killed a beautiful four-point—his first deer. Mario, happy for Todd, but envious over his beginner's luck, particularly in the face of his own hard luck over the years, arrived to assist with the buck. Neither had ever field-dressed a deer, and as it turned out, neither had a knife with him. Since they weren't too far from the vehicle, they drug the heavy buck down to the road and laboriously loaded it into the back of the little Chevy Citation they had come in. They then drove over to "Big Roy" Sheehan's house. Big Roy was a six-foot four-inch, 350 pound ex-cop and fellow Bible college friend. When Mario told him that Todd had killed a big buck and that it was in the back of their car, Big Roy came out to look at the deer wearing only his jockey shorts, since he was still sleeping when the knock came on his door. He was astounded upon seeing the buck—although, not so much at its size—and said, "You didn't gut it!" Because he was somewhat familiar with the care of a dead big-game animal, Roy was roped into the task of gutting the buck, as well as skinning it and cleaning it up. Of course, he went back in and got dressed first.

The next weekend Mario finally got to put his tag on a deer when he killed a blacktail doe during Oregon's Northwest Hunter's Choice Season, thereby ending many years of frustration.

A year later, Mario and his wife moved to Lewiston, Idaho where they presently reside, thus suspending Mario's comical pursuit of the elusive blacktail deer. In a recent telephone conversation with Mario, he told me that he has found mule deer to be as difficult to bag as either whitetails or blacktails. Apparently, car doors and speaker wires have been his latest obstacles while hunting, and he's still waiting to put a tag on his first buck. (Where is "Candid Camera" when we need them?)

# FALL 1986
# HUMBLED HUNTER

Changes in the big-game hunting regulations forced me to search for some new areas to hunt during the 1986 deer season. The Oregon Department of Fish and Wildlife moved the Cascade Elk Season from after the Western Oregon General Deer Season to October 18-26, causing the closure of deer hunting in all the blacktail units east of Interstate 5 during that time, except for deer hunters who also had an unused Cascade elk tag in their possession.

According to Biologist Dick Irish, of the ODFW's Springfield District Office, the Cascade Elk Hunt was moved from the later November period to mid-October in order to precede the snowfall that typically occurred before or during the later hunt; this snowfall caused the high-mountain Roosevelt Elk to move down into their wintering ranges where they were much more concentrated and, therefore, more vulnerable to hunters. It was hoped that moving the season ahead three weeks when the elk herds were in most cases more dispersed would allow more bulls—particularly spikes—to survive the hunting season. Although the ODFW anticipated the Cascade elk hunter success rate to fall considerably during the first year or two, it also hoped that the earlier season would eventually produce comparable harvest numbers to the November hunts of the past, but would include more mature bulls. Indeed, herd surveys conducted after that initial October elk hunt and in subsequent years indicated an increased bull to cow ratio and a higher percentage of branch-antlered bulls among many of the Cascade elk herds. Additionally, harvest numbers in subsequent years compared favorably to those of the later November hunts of the past. (ODFW Big Game Statistics 1986, 1987, 1993)

Beginning with the 1985 deer season, I did more and more of my hunting in the Getting's Creek area instead of at Lookout Point Reservoir. Another area I hunted numerous times during the 1985 and 1986 seasons was McGowan Creek, a tributary in the McKenzie River System, northeast of Eugene. Unfortunately, both Getting's Creek and McGowan Creek teem with hunters on the weekends. Luckily, however, a hunter like me, who is willing to get off from the road and into the brush, can find pockets where deer are plentiful and hunters are scarce. Of course with blacktails, having good numbers of deer present does not necessarily equate to seeing many deer.

I was again successful in drawing an antlerless/spike permit for the Dorena Unit, and on the first morning of the permit hunt, a warm, dry day which was the second Saturday of the general rifle season, Wayne Dale and I teamed up on a hunt at the top of Getting's Creek's north fork, several miles to the east of Saginaw, south of Eugene. The area we hunted in was part of a huge area which had been clearcut about nine years earlier—basically all of the land for miles across the top of the property formerly owned and managed by Georgia-Pacific, but subsequently purchased (in 1985) and managed by Weyerhaeuser. The north fork of Getting's Creek flowed through a shallow canyon from east to west in the section we were hunting. Its banks had various benches and small fingers populated mainly with seven-to eight-year-old Douglas firs, with blackberries and fern mixed in along with some alder and at the creek bottom, some willow. Because there was not much big timber anywhere for miles, the deer that lived in the area often bedded somewhere in the reforested clearcut. I figured if Wayne and I worked the top of each creek bank on opposite sides of the creek, we might jump a deer from its bed, possibly giving one or the other of us a shot as the deer fled from below the other hunter. I've jumped many blacktails from the upper part of a creek's bank over the years. When hunting alone, it's tough to get a shot because the scared deer usually jump down the bank away from me and then escape out the bottom of the creek, or up the other brushy bank not giving me a good, clear shot.

At shortly after ten in the morning, while Wayne and I worked downstream on opposite sides of the creek about seventy yards apart, I managed to get a stick poked into my right eye; it wasn't the first time that had happened. After sitting on a stump for about ten minutes to get over the injury, I decided I had better get to moving before Wayne grew impatient with me. We were not whistling there because we were able to keep track of each other's progress visually.

About a minute after continuing the hunt, I jumped a deer which I misjudged to be larger and shot it in the lungs at forty yards as it sneaked away at a broadside angle. Even though there was blood splattered all over the log and brush behind where the deer had stood when it was hit, the deer disappeared after my shot. I had no trouble finding it, however, as I followed its bright red blood-trail forty yards through the young firs and over a little ridge. Unfortunately, the deer was a fawn buck, which I tagged with my antlerless permit while swallowing my pride. I had made two mistakes which caused me to basically waste my extra tag on such a small deer. First, I failed to decide before the hunt exactly what size deer I would settle for. And second, I should have waited longer after poking my eye to allow my vision to return to normal. But since I didn't wait, I had no depth perception when I saw the deer; that caused me to misidentify it. Well, at least it didn't have spots!

As you might have guessed, Wayne rubbed it in at every opportunity, as did several other people we passed while driving out later in the morning. We placed a board over the fawn in the back of Wayne's truck to keep the sun off it, but I was accused of trying to hide the fact that I had killed Bambi.

During the nine-day-long Cascade elk season, I checked out a couple new deer hunting areas in the Siuslaw Unit which lies to the south and southwest of Eugene and to the west of Interstate 5. However, once the elk season was over, I immediately returned to hunting in the Indigo and Mckenzie Units, east of Interstate 5.

Though I saw numerous deer throughout the balance of the general season, I failed to get off a shot at any legal bucks. So again I went out to the Willamette Unit in November, testimony to the fact that I still had lots to learn about deer hunting.

In late November I passed up some small does while holding out for a buck, but unfortunately, I didn't see a buck and failed to fill my tag. It was the first time in six seasons that I had not killed at least a forked horn.

*What are you going to do? (ODFW Photo)*

# FALL 1987
# BACK ON TRACK

In 1987 the Oregon Department of Fish and Wildlife went a step further and closed all deer hunting in the Cascade Elk areas while the elk hunt—reduced to seven days—was in progress in mid-October. So as the deer season wore on, I decided to get serious about finding a good hunting spot in the Siuslaw Unit. That way, during the mid-season closure period east of Interstate 5, I would still have a quality place to hunt on the coast side of Interstate 5, which remained open during the Cascade elk hunt. Nowadays, I try to do a lot of my scouting prior to the season, but I didn't then. As it happened, I stumbled onto an area that I fell in love with immediately, which turned out to harbor many blacktails.

Because I continue to hunt this area at the time of my writing, I will be using fictitious names to designate specific locales, although I will concede that they are in the Siuslaw Unit, southwest of Eugene.

One of the reasons I developed a quick love affair with the new area in the Beaver Creek drainage was that it contained a large amount of prime blacktail habitat. What I consider to be a blacktail hot-spot always has some good stands of large fir—second-growth or old-growth—intermingled with plenty of maple, oak and alders. The big timber is bordered by young clearcuts containing young fir, madrone, alder, maple, cercocarpus (colloquially called "mountain mahogany," which henceforth I will call it), blackberries, and various other bushes that deer like to browse on. There is also a good water supply in the vicinity, i.e. springs or small creeks featuring plenty of alder, vine maple and even some cascara. The terrain is varied, consisting of steep hills, draws, ridges, flats, and benches, which give the deer necessary security, yet can be used to the hunter's benefit—particularly in letting him get close to deer or to gain an elevation advantage. Additionally, the area is not normally accessed easily, and the hunting pressure is very light.

Beaver Creek is parallelled for many miles by Beaver Creek Road, and much of the adjoining land is private. The remainder is public and managed by the Bureau of Land Management. Joining Beaver Creek Road at its upper end is Bell Road, which is several miles long, beginning in the bottom land of Beaver Creek and winding up in the low level hills. The creek bottom along Bell Road is populated mainly with oak and ash trees, with some alder, maple, cottonwood, and several patches of willow. Just off the bottom, alder, oak, maple and fir become prevalent, along with some cedar, and even a bit of pine. In the timbered areas of large fir, the ground cover is predominantly fern, with large patches of salal, Oregon Grape (the berries from both ripen in late summer and early fall and are good eating), and vine maple. Deer readily bed in any of these ground covering plants. Other potential bedding sights are next to the base of large standing trees, alongside large fallen trees, or particularly at the rootwad bases of downed timber.

A technique I utilize in hopes of spotting a bedded deer is to hike along below the ridgeline so as not to be sky-lighted, and yet be able to see a good-sized chunk of real-estate below me. Normally I can't see anything concealed directly beneath me. But by moving along the ridge, always on a deer trail, and looking over the canyon ahead of me or behind me, I can sometimes spot deer that I would never see right below me. The opposite side of a draw or canyon is a good place to spot bedded deer because the hunter has a good viewing angle. I mentioned earlier how I carry and use my binoculars in the timber. When hunting the bedding areas along steep hillsides, they are very useful. I always do a naked eye search first and then go back over the area looking for detail with my binoculars. In searching, I don't look for a whole deer, just for a part, something that doesn't fit the scenery. Even at that, bedded deer blend in so well that many times a hunter can look right at one and never notice it unless it flicks an ear or its tail. On a few occasions, I've spotted a deer standing and watched as it bedded down, and then I was either not able or barely able to see it even through my seven-power binoculars. It's no wonder that blacktails will so often just stay put while they watch a hunter move on past, oblivious to their presence.

The first year of hunting out Beaver Creek Road was an orientation time for me. I learned the lay of the land and found spots of good deer activity. One afternoon I hiked an old cat road off Bell Road and found a real nice area to hunt which I will call Scott's Canyon. I saw a couple deer on the way in and two more, in a different spot, on the way back out. This was in mid to late afternoon. There were several small clearcuts of varied age and plenty of fresh sign in the area as well. All of the key ingredients were present, so I knew I had something. Additionally, it was far enough off the beaten track, with tough enough access, that I doubted it was hunted by very many people.

After hiking back out from my initial venture into Scott's Canyon, I looked over a bit more of the landscape and then headed home at last light. While I was driving down the gravel road, a forked-horn came up out of a ditch into the road in front of me and then jumped back into the brush. About a mile farther down the road, a nice three or four-point did the same thing. Certainly that didn't hurt my enthusiasm level for this new area. To add to the thrill of that day's findings, the next morning while driving home from an early morning hunt off of Bell Road at around nine o'clock, I spotted a beautiful large-antlered four-point buck grazing in a farmer's field no more than sixty yards off the paved road. There was also a pair of does feeding up on a knoll about 100 yards to the right of the big buck. I stopped my car down the road from where the buck was feeding and seriously thought about shooting him, in spite of the fence between us. Fortunately, I gave in to my better judgment. After all, who would want to brag about a trophy buck that he road shot. That isn't even remotely sporting. Besides that, the risk of getting caught across the fence out in the field wasn't worth it. Anyway, after I watched the buck through my window for half a minute, the big boy got nervous and trotted away into the oak grove in the distance.

After not getting a forked-horn or better the previous year, I was determined to not let that happen again. Finding the area on Beaver Creek and seeing the number of deer I saw was very encouraging.

One day when I was hunting a section of timber to the north of Bell Road, just up off the creek bottom, I had worked over a small ridge and was sneaking along in an area containing a lot of madrone and oak when all of a sudden a bunch of deer burst from their beds about thirty yards ahead of me. They went everywhere. I counted at least five, but they were too fast, the brush was too thick, and I was too slow. Actually, when that many deer startle and run from close aboard, it is confusing. You want to look at all of them and end up not getting a good look at any of them. I've had the same thing happen several other times and have pretty well determined that when a number of deer are bedded together like that, it's generally going to be a bunch of does and fawns rather than any big bucks.

Throughout the remainder of the season, I continued to see or jump deer regularly while hunting in the new area in spite of bone-dry hunting conditions in the woods. (Some of the area was gated off for part of the season due to fire danger.) Then, on the third day of Hunter's Choice—Monday, November 2nd— I was hunting at daylight in the same area north of Bell Road in which I had jumped the group of bedded deer earlier. It was a damp morning with a light rain on and off. We had finally gotten some good rains in the previous week. After first light, I gradually worked up the slightly sloping ridge, going to the northwest and quartering the wind, which was out of the west. After going a couple hundred yards, I scared a deer off to my right. I got a quick look at it, but couldn't determine if it had antlers. As soon as it was out of my sight, the deer began the "blow routine." By that I mean it blew air out of its nose and mouth as a danger warning to other deer nearby. Many hunters call this snorting, but I've always called it blowing. The sound that I call snorting is deeper and raspier.

This blowing is a common reaction with deer, particularly for does with fawns close by. Many times I've seen the deer either before or after they did the blowing, and of those that blew which I got a good look at, not one was a buck. It is my belief that the air blowing is done much more commonly by does, but that younger bucks probably do it also. On the other hand, I believe that most older blacktail bucks do not vocally warn other deer around of an intruder. They are more likely to remain hidden or to sneak off without giving any hint of their presence. This is just my theory based on my own observations. Usually the deer will blow one breath lasting about three quarters of a second. Sometimes this is done only once, but often it is done several times at varying intervals ranging from several seconds apart to over a minute. A hunter can tell a deer has moved by the change in volume and often direction of the blowing sounds. I've heard two or more deer blow from different places around me, and I've heard the blowing routine go on for over five minutes. The longer span of blowing was always when I was hunting with one or two other people and we were some distance apart from each other. I believe in those instances the deer were more worried and confused about exactly where the danger was.

Two other sound signals of danger that deer use are stomping their feet while standing still or just before running off and also the aforementioned snorting. I've heard plenty of the foot stomping from blacktails, but rarely any snorting.

Back to the hunt. After scaring that deer, I continued along, crossed a ravine, and then reached an old moss-covered skid-road with an obvious game trail on it, which I began following to the west. When I still-hunt, I not only search ahead of me and to my sides, but also periodically behind me. Each step can open up a previously obscured sight lane and may reveal a deer not visible earlier. Rarely am I in any hurry to take my next step. Because of that, I often spot deer before they see me, which is what happened on this day. While inching along down the deer trail, I noticed a deer to my right and quietly released my safety, as I always do immediately upon seeing or hearing a deer. Even though I hadn't filled my general deer tag the previous year while holding out for a buck, my resolve to kill a buck had not wavered. I had no intentions of settling for a doe.

A moment later, the deer stepped out from behind some sparsely dressed vine maple about forty yards away and nibbled on some grass and ferns. As it slowly turned toward me, I saw a curved antler, betraying the fact that the deer was a buck. In some years before that and every year since, I would have considered passing that buck up for one with larger headgear. However, I was not going buck-less two years in a row, so I aimed for the center of the young buck's chest and shot just as he froze, the deer having finally sensed that something was amiss. Unfortunately for him, my shot was not a miss and down he went, killed instantly with a blown out heart and lung. When I got to him, I found he had a small, typical forked right-antler, but his left antler, still covered with velvet, grew stubbily, straight down beside his head, and was only about four inches long. He was a nice, fat deer, though small. I was very happy and relieved to have my buck, in spite of his being a very young one, probably only a year and a half old.

Ironically, late the next day—with only one day left in the Hunter's Choice Season—the Oregon Department of Fish and Wildlife announced that there would be a special three-day blacktail hunt on November 21-23 in all westside units. The reason for this was that the extremely dry weather thoughout much of the deer season had forced the extended closure of state-protected forest land and much land owned and managed by private timber companies during October to all recreational uses including hunting. Even in areas where hunting was allowed, conditions were so dry that few deer were taken. The Wildlife Department biologists were concerned that too many deer would be competing for a limited food supply during the winter. According to Fish and Wildlife Department spokesman Jim Gladson, "That could be a real problem when it comes to game damage to agricultural lands and timber lands." Ralph Denney, wildlife chief for the Fish and Wildlife Department, said that "biologists were unanimous in their belief that three days of hunting during the peak of the deer's mating season would be sufficient to attain the necessary harvest." (Eugene Register Guard 11-4-87)

Indeed, the additional three-day hunt did accomplish the ODFW's management goal of reducing blacktail numbers to a level in balance with the available food supply. Unfortunately, according to some sources, the late November hunt—which was hunter's choice in Northwestern Oregon and bucks only in Southwestern Oregon—took an extreme toll on the normally cautious older bucks due to the break in hunting pressure following the end of the regular deer rifle season and the fact that the rutting season was in full swing.

Local Eugene-area taxidermist Steve Erickson of Adam's Taxidermy told me:

> We had far more large, old bucks brought in here from that late hunt than we ever had before in a year. Taxidermists all over the state told us the same thing. And to pour salt on the wound [the wound of so many large, old bucks being killed], when I asked the ODFW if I could use a rifle like the other hunters—instead of my muzzleloader—during the three days when the special hunt overlapped our muzzle-loading season, they said, "No!"

I would have liked to have had a chance to hunt the later three-day season myself and been one of those lucky hunters who bagged a large, old buck.

# FALL 1988
# BUCK ON THE RUN

In 1988 I did a lot of my hunting in the Siuslaw Unit and particularly the area on Bell Road, learning more about the deer and land there. I also saw deer regularly, including some young bucks.

I recall one dry morning that I was hunting an area off of Bell Road with a friend from work named Steve, when as we were hunting along the upper edge of a timbered finger ridge, one of us jumped a deer from below and to the right of us. The deer ran off to our right out of sight and began blowing. Steve wanted to go after the deer, but I convinced him that to do so would be an effort in futility. From my experience, I knew that once a blacktail has been scared away, a hunter is very unlikely to get close enough for a shot by following after the deer. Everything is in the deer's favor at such times. Outwitting a blacktail deer is amply difficult without it having already been alerted to a hunter's presence. Steve's excitement and desire to go after the deer were typical of most blacktail hunters including myself, since many hours can be spent hunting without so much as hearing a deer, let alone seeing one.

As Steve and I continued our hunt around the mountain to the left that day, gradually working our way down to a more level flat, we scared a few more deer, a couple of which also blew the danger signal. Steve was thrilled with all the deer activity. Unfortunately, the dry conditions made it impossible to approach deer undetected.

Besides hearing the blow routine, we got to see just how close a blacktail buck will let a hunter get before it runs off. We were only about twenty yards apart—due to the brush situation and the lay of the land in that spot—when Steve froze and motioned to me that he could see a deer directly in front of him. I raised my rifle part way to my shoulder as I looked out ahead of him, but couldn't see any deer. The brush was very heavy all around us except for a narrow game-trail heading down hill to our right and ahead of us. A few seconds passed as I continued looking for the deer ahead of Steve. Finally, the deer jumped out from the thicket, no more than eight yards ahead of Steve, and in a flash disappeared down the trail ahead of me. Because I wasn't expecting it to be so close to Steve, I was taken by surprise when it finally spooked, though I doubt I would have shot it anyway. I wanted a large-racked deer.

Steve asked, "Did you see him?"

I answered, "Yeh, it was a forked-horn, but I was looking into the brush farther ahead of you and didn't expect it to be so close when it jumped out."

"I spotted him through the brush standing no more than twelve feet away and could see the tips of his antlers. But the brush was too thick for me to shoot him!" said Steve.

"I wouldn't have been able to shoot him from where I was either," I said.

The young buck's actions proved to be appropriate, and he lived to see another day, as did the several other deer we encountered that morning. At least we had a very enjoyable hunt together.

Friday morning, October 28th, found me in Scott's Canyon before daylight. As my previous hunting and scouting had shown me, Clearcut B had a special attraction for the deer because it had some secluded benches adjoined by a small, brushy creek and big timber to the south on a steep hill which provided good bedding sites. Actually, the entire area I call Scott's Canyon is outfitted nicely with good elevation changes, big timber, and feeding grounds in the open. One thing I especially liked about Clearcut B was the way its steep ground, combined with its benches, gave me the opportunity to approach close to deer without easily being detected. The brush and young firs were dense enough to provide a sense of security for the deer and yet sparse enough for me to often get a good look at any deer feeding in the unit or sneaking out ahead of me. One drawback to the lay of things at Clearcut B, however, was that the wind normally blew out of the west and, therefore, was at my back for part of the hunt. Fortunately, that didn't affect the area below me that I spent much of my time viewing while working sidehill to the east.

That morning I eased quietly through the patch of timber above Clearcut B, after having approached on the skid-road below Clearcut A which lies up hill from Clearcut B. Once I reached Clearcut B, I worked my way down the well-used deer trail which went downhill in the crease between two ridges and into the draw at the bottom. This trail was intersected by several other trails running horizontally on the hill side. I like to move along in natural creases in the land for three reasons: my movements and sounds (the noise I make) are concealed better and because deer favor such places for security. If I'm in the crease myself, I'm more likely to see deer that are hiding there. Conversely, I try to avoid moving along right on the top of ridges or out in the open on flats because my movements are much easier for deer to notice there. Additionally, when I need to take a sip from my canteen or eat a sandwich, I do it in a crease or draw, if possible, before going around a ridge into the next draw. If I'm going to have to make extra motion, I always try to do it in the least conspicuous spot I come to.

Getting to the first real good spot for scoping, about a third of the way down the crease and up to the left, I sat down and glassed the scantilly clad hill below me to the southwest across the tiny creek. The wind was blowing sporadically out of the west on the clear, temperate morning. After I had glassed for several minutes, a deer in the draw straight down the hill from me suddenly startled and ran, breaking a couple branches in the process. Instantly, I readied for a shot from my sitting position, but doubted the deer would come into the open as it could easily go downhill out the bottom of the draw and into the big timber instead. Fate was on my side, however, as the deer jumped the ravine and ran into the open, going away from me and up the next ridge. His antlers were obvious at once, so I aimed and shot. Getting no reaction from the buck which had turned to the right and was running uphill about 125 yards away, I aimed and fired again. He stumbled and then rolled downhill toward the ravine. Boy, was I pumped! I had seen multiple antler points and wanted to find out what he was, so I hurried down into the draw, crossed the creek, and climbed up the other bank. When I got to the buck, he was trying to get to his feet but could only get his front legs to stand beneath him. I was thrilled to see he was a nice four by four, minus eye-guards. Electing not to shoot him again, I drew my hunting knife, grabbed an antler, and cut his throat. Looking back I realize that shooting the buck would have been safer, and it would have killed the deer quicker. My second shot had hit him in the very front of the right ham, hit some bone, and then blown out his whole bowel system. It was a poorly-placed shot, probably because I hadn't led him.

The buck must have caught my scent on the morning's downhill thermal draft, but uncharacteristically for blacktail bucks, he bolted across an open ridge rather than holding tight or sneaking off down the draw. That mistake cost him his life. Against all other predators, this buck would have easily escaped unscathed. Why can't these deer figure out that they can't outrun a man's bullet? After field dressing my buck and making him into a "backpack," I carried him over three quarters of a mile—almost entirely uphill—to my rig. I was so proud of him that when I met a pair of deer hunters on the road while driving out, I stopped and showed him off. They were both clearly impressed. I guess I'm still a kid at heart, because I have a hard time keeping my excitement to myself. Poker, obviously is not my best game.

*Some trapping results*

# FALL 1989
# ANTLERS IN THE ALDERS

I opened the deer season, Saturday, September 30th, in the Coast Range Mountains, mainly because I was interested in continuing the fur prospecting I had been doing over the previous two weeks. Although it was a beautiful day weather-wise for deer hunting, meaning it drizzled all day long, I couldn't keep my mind focused on hunting. I had been locating an abundance of beaver and had given in to "trapping fever" even earlier than usual. The normal cycle of things goes like this for me: 1) My fishing rods come out of the shop and into the truck in the spring where they are available at my every whim and beckon. 2) Once deer season begins, the rods become dormant, and my rifle gets the call. 3) Finally, when deer season is over, my traps are activated and remain so throughout the winter.

My pre-season fur scouting paid off handsomely during the 1989-90 winter, as I set my single-season records for beaver and otter trapped with 167 and 11 respectively, not to mention the other critters that fell prey to my traps.

I didn't start getting serious about deer hunting until the third week in October, in spite of the fact we had a great fall with plenty of rain. Before deer season I scouted Scott's Canyon and liked what I found. In addition, I made a point to clear a bit of brush out of the way on a fifty-yard long shortcut along a deer trail through a dense, young fir lot on my way into the canyon. When packing out my four-point the previous year, I had noted that I could make the job easier by clearing some of the overhead brush in the shortcut area. Besides, getting some of the overhanging sticks and blackberry vines out of the trail would make for an easier pre-dawn commute there. As it turned out, the brush had closed in quite a bit more during the off-season, making my effort that much more worthwhile, assuming I scored again in Scott's Canyon.

Shortly before dawn on Saturday, October 28th, I hiked into Scott's Canyon; my destination was Clearcut B, where I had killed the four-point on the same date a year earlier. Enroute, I scared a large-bodied deer in the dimly-lit heavy-fog at the bottom of Clearcut A. I kicked myself for not noticing the deer first. But because my objective was to be at Clearcut B when the day dawned, and since I couldn't hunt every unit at prime time, I couldn't worry about any deer that I encountered in the dark on my way in. I've had the same thing happen at other times when hiking to my first light's position. It has always frustrated me, and I think that is one definite advantage that evening stand hunts have over morning stand hunts. Normally, any deer the evening hunter scares are frightened <u>after</u> he has finished his hunt rather than before it. Even being on stand an hour before daylight is no guarantee that the morning hunter won't scare deer from his ambush point because deer feed and move throughout much of the night. Deer movement at dusk, on the other hand, is much more likely to be confined to a predictable time—the last hour or less of daylight.

I made the same approach to Clearcut B as I had on several other occasions including the previous year. Earlier in the season, I had seen does, fawns, and even a couple of spikes in the unit but so far no branch-antlered bucks. I knew the rut was beginning soon because I had seen some freshly rubbed trees in the last week. That caused my anticipation to be greater than earlier in the year. (Unlike whitetail deer, blacktails do not make ground scrapes to mark their rutting territory or to set up meeting places for themselves and estrous does—at least I've never seen any. They do, however, rub on and spar with trees within their rutting zone.) It was cool and mostly cloudy with intermittent fog as I glassed the unit across the draw while the sun sneaked over the horizon in the east. No deer were visible.

Most of the time I don't like to have fog in the area I'm hunting because it obscures so much from my sight. There are times, though, when fog can be used to a hunter's advantage, such as when he must cross an open area to get into closer range or to get in a better position for seeing or shooting deer that are active on a hillside above him. This, however, was not one of those times.

Sitting in the same spot where I shot the buck from the previous year, I waited for the fog to clear, which it did within twenty minutes. Around 8:30 I heard a vehicle drive along the gravel road over the hill behind the timber that adjoined Clearcut B to the south. A few minutes later, I observed three hunters come over the ridge about 300 yards away from me to my right, at the upper, western end of Clearcut B; they glassed the upper portion over. Of course, they couldn't even begin to see most of the area I was hunting.

Numerous times over the years, I've been down in a clearcut watching deer while some road-hunters slowly cruised by above me totally ignorant of the activity transpiring below them. (I don't want to imply that the hunters mentioned above were necessarily road-hunters.) Generally, the obscured deer paid little or no attention to the passing vehicles. However, if a rig stopped, and particularly if a door could be heard opening or closing, the deer immediately froze and concentrated fully on the activity above them. In cases where the deer were plainly in the open, they stood like statues many times at just the sound of the passing vehicle. Interestingly, most of the deer I've seen in clearcuts when hunting season was closed did not appear to be as concerned about human activity nearby. Deer seem to be able to sense when they are in danger from man, and they behave accordingly.

After several minutes, two of the hunters across the way from me returned to their concealed vehicle and waited for their comrade, whom I could still see, to answer nature's call. Theirs was the first vehicle I had heard there in three seasons; although I knew the road was up there, I had assumed it was gated off. Later I would find out that it was, in fact, gated but that these locals had a key to it. Whether or not they had permission to be using the road, I never knew.

When the third hunter disappeared over the ridge and I heard the vehicle leave, I decided to work on around the hill I was on to the east side-hill and gradually work my way down into the bottom near the creek. I had used this strategy before. This particular clearcut has a lot of mountain mahogany in it, and the deer were browsing noticeably on it. They had numerous trails going in and out of the brush patches and following

along the various benches and creases. It took me most of an hour to round the part of the mountain facing south. I had worked down to about 100 yards away from the very young alders lining the creek bottom separating the timber across the way from the hill I was on. Along my way, there was plenty of brush to conceal me from animals above, as well as to keep me from being sky-lit to animals below me. To the left of the big timber across from me was an older reprod unit of eight-to ten-year-old firs on a steep hill.

At about ten o'clock I heard some noise like a walking deer in the timber across the way and below me. I had spotted deer there before, but never a shootable buck. At once, I focused my attention in the direction of the sound and spotted a very nice buck with a large, wide rack. Not taking the time to count points, I immediately raised my rifle to shoot. Unfortunately, this buck was stepping right out—nose to the ground and obviously in hot pursuit of a doe—and reached the cover of the alder-laden creek bottom in the second it took me to ready myself. When he dropped down into the ravine and out of sight, I figured I could get a shot at him coming up out of the draw on my side, but I wasn't in the right place for a shot. I was at least fory-five feet above him, besides an overland distance of over sixty yards, with a knoll between me and where I guessed he would come up. Hurriedly, I moved about twenty feet farther down the hill to the left and readied my sights for him. When he didn't appear in a few seconds, I wondered where he had gone. At that instant I saw him out of the corner of my left eye going through the alder brush on my side of the creek, but farther downstream than I had anticipated. I swung my rifle a few inches to the left, and as soon as I had the very front of him centered in my crosshairs, I pulled the trigger. He was gone! I ran a little farther down the hill, stopping on a rise that allowed me to see a fair chunk of ground across the adjoining spring which ran in from the timber to my north, behind me to the left. The buck had headed in that direction.

That little confluence between the mountains is the epicenter of the whole surrounding area—a great deer funnel. Every year buck rubs can be found on the alder trees in that little hole.

When the buck did not show, I was somewhat concerned because he certainly could have slipped through into the timber at the junction without crossing into the clear ground I was watching. On the other hand, not seeing him could be a great sign. I hurried down to his position at the moment of my shot. Searching hopefully, I found him lying dead in the alders with a hole through his neck. I could not believe my eyes! He was a beautiful full-pointed five by four, sporting nice eye guards to boot! His rack had close to a fifteen-inch inside spread. During all of my previous years of blacktail hunting, I had considered a five-point blacktail buck to be almost a mythical creature. I also knew that very few hunters had ever shot one—at least not in the lowlands—so he was a very rare prize indeed. (Certainly one can not compare the higher, Cascade blacktails with the ones in the lowlands because many of the higher country blacktails have mule-deer genes mixed in.) Two years in a row I had killed my buck on October 28th. I am always more optimistic when hunting on the date of a previous kill, probably because on those days I often re-think and re-live in my mind the earlier successful experience.

After gutting the big buck and getting him up hill to my truck which was over a mile away, I hurriedly drove home with him. On the drive home, I turned repeatedly to get a look at my trophy in the back of the truck. Numerous times I also gave into my excitement and shouted, "Alright! Thank you God!" while pumping my fist in the air. This behavior is typical for me each year upon harvesting my buck. Maybe you can relate? When I stopped at Dad's to show him my trophy, he looked into the back of my truck and said, "I don't know how you do it!" To be honest, I think I'm probably far more lucky as a blacktail hunter than skillful. The old saying, "You can't catch a fish if your line is not in the water," can be applied to hunting in the sense that you have to be in the woods to get lucky enough to kill a buck. In my case, I've spent enough time in the woods to know where I need to be for mother luck to smile upon me regularly.

This five-point buck was definitely in the rut on October 28th, which is earlier than some hunters believe happens. The next year further confirmed to me the fact that in some years blacktails certainly will be in the rut before the end of October.

*A trophy in anyone's book*

# FALL 1990
# CHEWING THE CUD

The season opened on September 29th, a cool, wet, overcast day. For the first time, I opened the season in Scott's Canyon. At first light, I saw a couple of does near the top of Clearcut B, but no bucks. Using the same strategy I had successfully employed the year before, I moved around the mountain to the east, gradually working downhill, while paying particular attention to the areas above and below me. Unfortunately, the wind was blowing out of the west at a good clip. The brush in the clearcut had grown considerably—blackberries, mountain mahogany, and madrone being the main culprits—giving the deer more concealment. When I was about halfway around the ridge, suddenly a very nice, wide-antlered buck jumped out of a thick patch of mountain mahogany about thirty-five yards ahead of me and downhill to my left. I raised my rifle up in his direction at once, but he bounced over a rise straight out to my left about forty yards away. Knowing the lay of the land and that I might still be able to get a shot, I ran toward the brushy rise in hopes of gaining elevation in order to see him.

It has been my experience with big bucks that they normally only bounce far enough to get to where they feel safe, and then they slow to an even gait or a trot and finally a fast walk. Therefore, if a hunter can get to a point where he will get a good look at a fleeing buck, he can sometimes get a shot. That was not in the cards for me on this day, though, as I slipped on the muddy downhill slope and fell hard, flat on my back, sliding several feet down the hill while my rifle lay out of my reach a foot uphill from me, pointing up the hill. Needless to say, the buck got away. The worn out soles on my boots were largely to blame. Several days later I slipped on some frosty ground while walking down a hill hunting and ended up flat on my back again. I finally wised up and got some new boots after the second spill. Never again will I try to get by with wornout boots when hunting. After each mishap I shot my gun to ensure that it was still on target, which it was.

I didn't realize I had injured my right knee when I fell opening morning until three days later, when after walking extensively on it while searching for mushrooms in the Cascade Mountains, it became very sore. Over the ensuing three weeks while mushroom picking and deer hunting, that knee proved to be a definite liability and at times a source of extreme pain. One day in the Cascades, I even had to splint it up with sticks at hand in order to get back out to the road. I was forced to take a number of days off from picking to allow it to rest.

On Thursday October 25th, a temperate, dry day, I began hunting at daylight at another favorite area off Bell Road called Billy Butte. Although we had received some rain a few days earlier, conditions for still-hunting were not the best. I hunted down through a 300-yard-long patch of second-growth fir on the top of the butte, working to the west into the wind, without any luck. At about 9:30 I reached the western tip of the southern-most finger-ridge, where oak and maple trees made a good showing among the large firs. I opted to hike down the left edge of the ridge a ways and then work sidehill to the north and to my right. Since this end of Billy Butte had a few little fingers separated by fairly steep draws, I figured at that time of morning I would stand a good chance of seeing some deer along the side of the fingers. If nothing else, maybe I would spot or jump a bedded buck and get a shot as he went around the opposite ridge.

There was no way that I could move silently because of the partially dried oak and maple leaves scattered liberally on the ground. However, by moving at my normal snail's pace, and only occasionally crackling a leaf, I didn't expect that my sounds would disturb a deer too much. After all, dry leaves were falling out of the trees around me periodically and making more noise than I was as they crunched each time they hit a branch or other dry leaves on their patient descent to the ground. After hunting along sidehill for about fifteen minutes, I spotted something gray twenty-feet downhill and about forty-five yards to my right, ahead of me, that instantly registered in my brain,

"a bedded deer!" Immediately, I eased my safety off while fluidly raising my rifle to my shoulder.

I had an antlerless/spike permit in addition to my buck tag, so I could legally take any deer I saw. But I had already decided before dropping over the top of the ridge twenty minutes earlier not to shoot anything but a large-antlered buck from that point on in my hunt. My thinking was that I could fill my special permit closer to a road, and there was no reason to work any harder than I had to in packing my extra deer a longer distance or up a steep grade. I will gladly kill and pack out a large buck from anywhere, but I choose not to do that with does and small bucks. The lower part of Scott's Canyon is another example of a place where I had earlier elected not to shoot anything but a big buck.

When I looked through my scope—which was set on three power—I almost couldn't believe my eyes. A beautiful buck with antlers wider than his ears was looking up at me while chewing his cud. He was bedded beneath some lightly foliated hazel-nut branches a few yards beyond the crotch dividing the two finger ridges. Unfortunately, there was a medium-sized fir tree between us which partially obscured the buck's body. My heart raced as I took three gentle steps backwards to open a good shooting lane, while cranking my scope up a bit and praying that the buck would not move. As soon as I had a clear shot at the front part of the buck's body, I aimed into his rib cage and fired. He staggered to his feet at once, took about three steps and went down. I approached him slowly but saw his efforts to get up were fruitless. A shot to his upper neck finished him off. He was a four by three with eye guards and nearly a seventeen-inch inside spread on his main beams. A beauty. My shot had hit his liver. After field dressing him, I packed him out sidehill and downhill about a mile to the gravel road I had driven in on. I then stashed the buck and walked the road uphill to my truck. My bum knee, well rested and aided by a knee brace, came through for me with no problems that morning.

Five days later, on the 30th, a foggy, drizzly day, I went back out to hunt the top of Billy Butte where my antlerless/spike permit was valid. At dawn I hiked the short distance through the clearcut bordering the large timber on the western end of Billy Butte and then worked my way down through the middle of the second-growth fir forest that also had a number of maple and cedar trees. It was a hunter's dream day weather-wise except for the fog that periodically moved in and out of the timber.

At 8:30, as I was easing slowly and silently along on the mossy forest floor, a doe came trotting into view from behind some dense cedar trees on my right, no more than twenty yards away. A buck was right on her flank, his nose seemingly glued to her extended tail. Like a couple of love-sick teenagers, they were oblivious to my presence. Immediately, I could see the buck had three points on his light-beamed right antler, but surprisingly, his left antler was merely a long curved spike. Both deer trotted to the left in front of me, made a u-turn in my direction and then went back to my right, stopping about fifteen yards away. I immediately dropped the doe with a head shot. Amazingly, the buck did not run off, but ran only about forty yards away from me and acted as though he wanted to come back. I watched him closely through my scope. He had the "hots" and did not want to leave, even when I walked towards him. Finally, after over a minute, I ran at him and yelled. At last, he got the message that this doe would not be available anymore that day or ever again, so he left.

Out of curiousity, I later called up the Oregon State Police and asked the game officer if I could have legally killed the three-by-spike to fill my antlerless/ spike tag. After deer season I had noticed in the Big-Game Regulations that an elk with branched antlers on one side, but only a spike on the other side, fit the legal definition (as diagrammed) of "spike" for the spike-only elk areas. The game officer confirmed that I indeed could have legally filled my spike permit with the odd-antlered buck. You better believe I chided myself for not knowing that earlier. His rack would have made a unique addition to my collection.

*He was bedded in the wrong spot*

# FALL 1991
# LIMITED OPPORTUNITIES

    I became a full-time, single parent to my three-year-old son Cody and my thirteen-month-old daughter Tasha in April 1991. Adding to my heartbreak and burden was the fact that my three-year-old son had recently been found to be legally blind and diagnosed with a degenerative retinal disease. Like every other parent, I wanted the road of opportunities to be limit-less for my children, but that is no longer possible. As an example, I will never be able to experience the joy of showing Cody how to hunt and then share in his excitement at killing his first deer. I still grieve over his visual limitations. As a result of my increased parental responsibilities, my outdoor activities—particularly hunting and fishing—became limited. When deer season came around, I was hard-pressed to get out very much at all, which frustrated me to no end. Knowing my opportunities to hunt would be limited, I decided before the season to settle for any three-point or better that I saw. I was very fortunate that my step-mother and Dad were very supportive during such a trying time in my life and pitched in several times to watch the kids for me.

    On opening morning, September 28th, a warm dry day, I returned to Scott's Canyon and Clearcut B. I figured it would be my last opening morning there, because everything had grown up so much since killing the four-point three years earlier. In much of the unit, deer would be very difficult to see, let alone get a shot at. At daybreak I was sitting in the same spot from where I had shot the four-point, glassing the unit. It wasn't long before I heard some deer feeding in the draw below where the four-point buck had fallen when hit. I could hear the deer pushing around in the blackberry vines, as well as snapping limbs underfoot. I could even hear them ripping foliage off of tree branches and blackberries. Focusing my attention in the direction of the sounds, I strained to pick out any deer forms or movement in the thick, young firs and flourishing alders. Unfortunately, some madrone and maple trees between the draw and me had grown to such an extent that they screened a portion of the opposite ridge and a lot of the draw from my view. Continuing to listen to the deer a hundred yards away, I finally spotted one as it climbed out of the draw and up the opposite bank below me. I got a slight case of the shakes. Settling myself down with some slow deep breaths, I cranked my scope up to six-power to help me distinguish through the surrounding branches whether the deer had antlers or not. It didn't.

Although I use my binoculars to scan over an area and to search for detail when looking for deer, once I know a deer is present, as in this case, I will normally use my rifle scope for specifically targetting an animal. The reason, of course, is that in the heavy brush that is so typical of blacktail country a deer may only be in an open shooting lane for a second or two before disappearing out of sight for good. If I'm still looking through my binoculars at that one opportune moment, I've missed my only chance to shoot the deer. I've talked with many a hunter who said that if only he had been looking at a deer through his rifle scope instead of looking through his binoculars or even watching the deer with his naked eyes, he could have shot it before it got into the brush. The same thing has happened to me. On the other hand, if I spot a bedded deer or one that is obviously standing still unaware of my presence, I will often look it over thoroughly with my 7X binoculars before deciding to raise my rifle up on it.

Several seconds later, a second deer came partially into the clear, joining the one I was already watching, and I recognized antlers immediately. Although I could see that its rack was not as large as the previous year's four-point, I made out at least three points on each antler. I followed the buck's body as best I could as he milled around in the fir and alder, quite sure I would get a good clear shot eventually. My heart was beating loudly, but I held steady with my left arm braced on my knee in a sitting position. Finally, the buck moved to the right and came into a small opening. My rifle kicked at the sound of the shot, as I held just behind his right shoulder. He vanished. One deer took off to the buck's right and disappeared into the alders and blackberries that engulfed the draw. As I hustled down and reached the ravine, I saw another deer run off to the left through the heavy brush and go around the ridge. I dropped down, crossed the creek, and climbed up the opposite bank, and had no trouble finding the exact spot where the buck had stood at the instant I shot because I had noted the large stump just up the hill from him. Unfortunately, he was nowhere around, nor was there any sign of a hit. I spent a long time searching the brush, ravine, and ground in hopes of finding blood, but with no luck.

Later, I shot my rifle to see where it hit. I found that it was hitting over six inches high at 100 yards. Since the buck I shot at was 125 yards away, my bullet would have hit at least seven inches higher than where I aimed, easily accounting for my miss. The mistake I made when sighting in my gun a week earlier was that I took the kids and an impatient young hunting friend along. My friend kept firing off rounds, and the kids kept fussing, while I was trying to concentrate on getting my sights tuned up. I never was satisfied, but became weary of the racket and quit shooting before I should have. I won't make that mistake again.

On Thursday evening, October 24th, a cold, windy day with intermittent rain and partial clearing, I stood silently under the shade of a large fir tree on the top of Billy Butte as daylight slipped away. Before daybreak I had driven up to the Crescent Lake area in Oregon's Central Cascades in search of mush-rooms but had found four plus inches of snow from over night on the ground, precluding any mushroom picking. Still, I hiked around on the hills above the lake for a couple hours, partly be-cause I loved breathing the fresh mountain air and enjoyed the serenity of the quiet, white-covered lodgepole-pine forest. After returning to my truck and driving home, arriving in early after-noon, I ate lunch and headed out to the Beaver Creek area to hunt the last three hours of daylight. While hunting around in the oak, fir and cedar along Billy Butte's rocky south ridge, I bent down to look under some trees out ahead of me, and I spotted a deer's legs, lower body, and head visible below an oak tree's foliage about forty-five yards away. The deer was looking right at me, its head only a few inches off the leaf- covered ground. When I raised my rifle, the deer ran off and began blowing the danger sign. I hadn't determined if it had antlers, though it was not a large animal judging by what I did see. Over the next half hour, while continuing to work the rocky mountain-top, I jumped that same deer—I guessed—two more times without seeing it, and it blew at me each time.

Ultimately, as dark approached, I took position under the big fir tree. With my back to the bark, I watched an area under some oak and fir trees thirty yards away across a rocky, grass-covered knoll. Twenty minutes later, a deer appeared like a ghost, upwind from me, in the shade across the way. It was half-heartedly picking at some grass as it worked its way toward a nearby clearcut. Because of how little light there was, I had to crank my scope up to 4.5 power to see the deer's head well enough to make sure it was not a forked horn. I could legally shoot anything I saw because I had drawn an antlerless/spike permit for that area, but I wanted either a doe, spike, or a 3-point or better buck. As I tried to determine what, if anything, the deer had for head-gear, my scope fogged up from my breath. Quickly, I wiped it clear with the tissue from my front shirt pocket, and when I was satisfied the deer did not have antlers and was not a fawn, I pulled the trigger. At the gun's report, the deer lay kicking, dead within seconds. I ran over and found that the deer was actually a yearling, nubbin-spike buck instead of a doe. After I dressed him out by flashlight, I drug him the 100 yards to the road I was parked on. I knew I would be doing more dusk-time stand hunting in the future. Over the years, I have done the bulk of my hunting during the morning hours.

On Saturday, October 26th, a cloudy day with intermittent light rain, I drove out to Bell Road to hunt below Billy Butte. At the western base of the finger extending from Billy Butte, just to the north of where I killed the big buck a year earlier, was what I believed to be an excellent deer funnel. It is a natural geographical intersection for any deer travelling from north to south, or vice versa, because the steep finger forces the animals to pass by way of the wooded flat at the base of the mountain's point. Additionally, the nearby clearcuts of varying age with their succulent flora, in combination with the many deciduous trees in the flat, make that tract—which I call Murphey's Funnel—a high activity area. It is the ideal transition zone and an excellent location for a stand. To add to my anticipation, I had found two nice three-point antlers of different configurations—one that looked more like a whitetail's than any I'd ever found—on the main deer trail in the Funnel a few days earlier. Finding the antlers was one of the things that really got me to stop and analyze the set-up in the first place. And when I did, everything made perfect sense. All the ingredients were there.

As fate would have it on the morning of the 26th, circumstances caused me to leave home later than I planned. I had wanted to be on stand at first light at a ground blind at the base of a downed old-growth fir tree overlooking several choice trails at Murphey's Funnel. The funnel is a three-quarter mile trek from the road I park on. To reach it I would have to walk through the initial young clearcut, then through a 200-yard-wide oak grove, cross a spring, hike uphill through a privately owned, medium-sized clearcut (I call it Clearcut B), and finally get to the mixed fir and hardwood lot adjoining the Funnel. Since it was already light by the time I reached Clearcut B, I moved through it at a slow, steady pace looking it over for any possible deer as I went. My objective, though later than I desired, was still to get to Murphey's Funnel. I never made it.

About a third of the way through the clearcut, as I was passing a thick section of varied brush on my right, a three-point buck opted to leave the security of that brush and do a high-step, tip-toed escape through the knee-high blackberries and ferns to my right. He was only thirty yards away as I immediately zeroed in on his ribs just behind his right shoulder and shot. He showed no sign of damage and zigzagged back to the left farther away from me. I shot the same spot on his left side. Still giving no indication of being hit, he apparently had had enough of my target practice and began hopping over a bunch of blackberries and stray branches leftover from the earlier logging, going away from me on the little ridge to the northwest. When he got out to about sixty yards away, he turned right and trotted down into a brushy draw. I got one more shot at his right shoulder just before he disappeared down the blackberry-laden draw to the right. At once, I moved over to my right in hopes of getting another shot at him in the blackberry infested draw, but didn't see him. I couldn't understand how I could have missed him at that close range. Without delay, I picked my way through the brush to the point where I last saw him. He was lying ten feet down the blood-slickened slope, having finally acknowledged me as the winner. All three of my shots had hit their mark, destroying both lungs in the process, and exited out the other side of the buck's body. Fortunately, there was very little meat damaged. This odd-horned three-point (with fairly good antler mass), which I guessed to be three and a half, demonstrated that as I said earlier only a young, foolish buck would attempt a tip-toed sneak-away through the open in plain sight of a hunter. An older buck most likely would have held tight and blended in behind the brush, letting me pass without incident.

# FALL 1992
# MURPHEY'S FUNNEL

My stepmother, Rosella, passed away a few weeks before deer season after a six-month battle with liver cancer. She was a good grandmother to my kids and pitched in to watch them on numerous occasions. Because of Rosella's absence during the 1992 deer season, I was forced to pay a babysitter many of the times I hunted. The biggest drawback to taking the kids to a sitter was that I could rarely get out by first light or stay until dusk because of the sitter's hours, so I missed the two half-hour periods of greatest potential. Furthermore, I had to look at my deer hunting as good and necessary exercise and worthwhile therapy in order to justify forking out so much in child-care expenses while I hunted. Dad took Cody overnight on Fridays a number of times while a couple different lady friends took Tasha. That freed me up for some early morning hunts on several Saturdays.

During the previous summer, I had replaced the Bushnell 3X9 scope on my 30.06 with a brand-new Tasco 2.5-10 power scope. The new scope is an improvement over the old scope in several ways. 1) It gathers light better, allowing me to see better in low light situations like at dusk. 2) It has very little glare. (I can look almost directly into the sun and still see clearly.) I lost chances at several deer with the old scope due to sun glare. 3) It has a wider field of view—particularly with the 2.5 setting—which is especially important for close range action in the timber I typically hunt. Aside from the new scope's advantages, the main reason I purchased it was that one year in the past my old scope fogged up on the inside while I was hunting in cold weather—that after hunting in heavy rains for several days—and from then on, I always worried it would fog up again in rainy or cold weather. Luckily it never did fog again, but neither did I ever have complete peace of mind. I should have replaced it earlier but put it off. I'm happy with the new scope; it's definitely a better one. Now what I need to get is a good bolt-action rifle to replace my auto-loader, which, frankly, doesn't group very well.

Opening morning, October 3rd, found me and a friend from church, Tim Watson, hooking up to hunt an area in the Siuslaw Unit that I will call Wygle Mountain. It was the first time since 1988 that I had hunted with anyone. Tim, a full-time staff member with Campus Crusade For Christ at the University of Oregon, is a veteran big-game hunter. All of my past hunting partners except my Uncle Ed Vohs moved out of Lane County, some out of Oregon, which is one reason why I had not hunted with anyone in several years. No, I don't drive them away. Actually I think everybody I ever hunted with would say they enjoyed hunting with me, just as I enjoyed their partnerships. But because I like the flexibility and solitude of hunting deer alone, I don't seek out partners. In fact, I've probably offended some people when I didn't take them up on their offers to hunt together.

In spite of the great hunting weather for an opening day— intermittent light rain—Tim and I didn't see any deer all day, though we both jumped some. In the morning, we heard a number of shots in the surrounding area, possibly indicating that some other hunters were having better luck than we were. I did find a very weathered four-point antler, so at least we had some fuel for daydreaming. It was the first opening morning in years that I didn't see a deer.

Over the first two and a half weeks of the season, I did all of my hunting in the proximity of Wygle Mountain, mostly in an area that Tim and I named "The History Hole." There were plenty of deer in the area, but sightings proved to be much less common than in the Beaver Creek drainage. I attributed it to the fact that there was considerably more hunting pressure and human activity there. One Saturday, I even spotted a couple of the local Army Guard's jeeps parked in the area, evidence that a field exercise was being conducted in the vicinity. So much for undisturbed deer hunting. There were four main reasons why I kept going back to the History Hole: 1) I liked the lay of things; 2) there was a large amount of deer sign—including well-used deer trails, numerous deer droppings, plenty of pre-season buck rubs and numerous deer beds; 3) It provided me a new area of scenery which, of course, was stimulating; 4) I happened to find a non-typical five-point antler on one of my first few hunts. I knew the odds of my seeing the previous owner of the antler were slim, but I couldn't help but hope for a meeting, anyway.

Another feature that added to my pleasure while hunting the History Hole was the thriving silver-gray squirrel population in a several-acre oak stand nearby. Using my binoculars, I enjoyed watching the squirrels scamper about picking up acorns and climbing up and around the oak trees. Squirrels don't seem to do anything fluidly. Each move they make is a nervous jerky motion, reminding me of the old black and white movies which seem to skip with every frame.

Later in the season, I returned to Bell Road for some of my hunting, where I saw deer every time I went out. The regular blacktail season was to remain open through November 11th, the latest date of all the years I have hunted. Therefore, I knew I would have some prime hunting during the early part of the rut.

Some people I have talked to over the years who hunt Eastern Oregon's mule deer year after year don't think it is fair that they get only seven to twelve days to hunt while blacktail hunters generally have thirty-five to forty days to fill their tags, not counting the extended Willamette Unit hunt. When I invite them to join us on the west side, however, they often answer with something like this:

> There's no way that I'm going to beat the heavy brush on this side of the mountain looking for deer! I tried it a few different years and got soaked, scratched up, and hardly ever saw a deer. I see more deer in half a day of hunting in Eastern Oregon than I ever saw in a whole season over here hunting puny blacktails.

My answer, "That's why we have such a long season over here." In spite of the long season, only a minority of Oregon's blacktail hunters fill their tags in any given year. (ODFW 1993 Big Game Statistics) In fact, only a low percentage of west-side hunters consistently kill a buck. Furthermore, only a very small portion of blacktail hunters fill their tags year after year with older, branch-antlered bucks. A person who questions the need for a long blacktail season need only spend a few days searching for a blacktail buck to realize the difficulty involved in simply seeing one, let alone getting a good shot at one.

On the evening of October 31st, I filled my antlerless/spike tag with a doe on the top of Billy Butte. I watched her milling around in the big timber for over twenty minutes from my ground stand before deciding, on the spur of the moment, to shoot her at last light. I had passed up some earlier does and two spikes with up to three-inch-long antlers, while holding out for a larger spike or maybe even a spike-by-fork. Nevertheless, I finally decided to get the special tag filled so I could concentrate fully on getting a big buck.

Throughout the previous spring and summer, there had been an extensive amount of logging in the areas along Bell Road. Unfortunately, two of the places where I had killed bucks in the timber in the vicinity of Billy Butte had been clearcut. I wasn't happy about that—as I wasn't happy in the past when many of the other timbered areas I had jumped or killed deer in were logged off, many of my memories going along with the big trees—because there was getting to be a real shortage of older timber remaining there. I think the Northern Spotted Owl situation, along with a large segment of the public's push for dramatic logging cutbacks, has many private timber-land-owners worried that if they don't log their lands now, they won't be able to in the future. High property taxes on standing timber certainly is another factor forcing land-owners to log and sell their timber just to be able to keep up with their tax payments. With the price timber has been selling for in recent years and the real threat landowners face of being unable to liquidate their assets in the future, it's not hard to sympathize with those owners who have chosen to log as much as they can now, while they still can, whether I agree with it or not.

November 7th, an overcast Saturday morning, was the first day of the Hunter's Choice season, which was in effect for the final five days of the general rifle season. I had waited all season long to take my stand at Murphey's Funnel below Billy Butte. Since a year earlier, when I killed my buck on the way

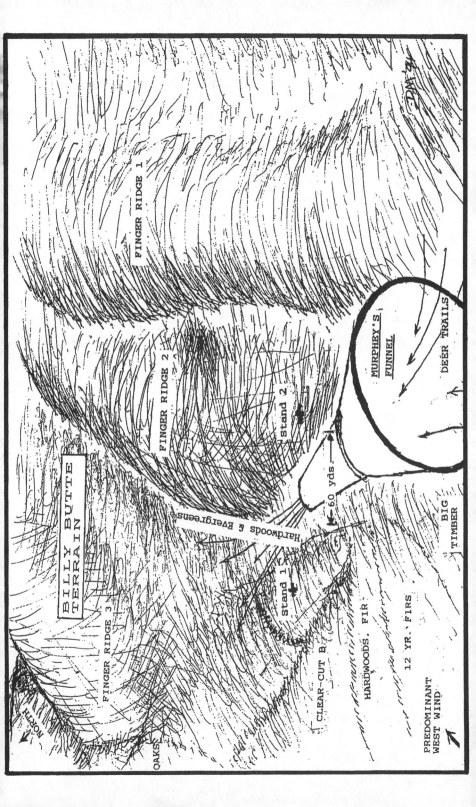

up to the Funnel, I had intended to take a stand there sometime during the last week of the 1992 blacktail season if I hadn't filled my tag before then. I felt that the Funnel would be the ideal spot to ambush a big buck during the early rutting season.

While I hiked in the dark through the first clearcut before the oak grove on my way up to Murphey's Funnel, a deer did the "blow routine" in the timber above me. I'm sure that I was the object of its agitation. After hiking through the oak grove by flashlight and crossing the spring, I reached the bottom of Clearcut B just as dawn was breaking. I then moved up through the clearcut, stopping periodically to glass the unit over with my binocs. Minutes after first light, I began hearing gunshots regularly from all across the Beaver Creek valley. The barrage continued throughout the morning, and I knew many does and fawns were biting the dust. I know that some hunters do very little hunting before the Hunter's Choice season begins and then go out and kill a doe or fawn. As long as the blacktail population continues to thrive and there continues to be a Hunter's Choice season, I'm sure the practice will continue.

Twenty minutes after daybreak, I reached my predetermined point near the top of Clearcut B where I could move into the timber below the knoll adjoining Murphey's Funnel. Immediately after entering the timber, I began working gradually around the knoll which bordered the northwest end of the Funnel. The wind was very slight out of the northwest as I moved to the east. I wasn't too concerned about being on my spot any earlier, because I knew that with the rutting season on, the bucks would be chasing around throughout the day in search of any estrous does. The leaves on the ground were wet and soft as I inched my way quietly around the knoll. Below and to my left was a small flat or valley. Maple and alder trees were abundant among the large fir trees throughout the whole vicinity of Murphey's Funnel. I looked over the flat below me and all of the area I could see, including that ahead of me to the east, as I worked toward the Funnel where I anticipated the most activity to occur. Twenty minutes after entering the timber, a fawn startled from thirty yards directly below me. It must have been obscured by a large tree because I had been glassing the whole area over carefully and had not seen it. I watched as it slowly tip-toed away to my left, finally going out of sight a couple minutes later.

Ten minutes more passed and I was only thirty yards from my destination, stand one, able to see the intersecting trails I wanted to watch, when I heard a limb snap to my right in the Funnel area. Immediately, I eased my safety off and got to the ready because I knew that sound from too many times before. A deer was coming my way. I heard some more noise, and then a doe came out of the brush uphill to my right about forty-five yards away and passed by forty yards in front of me. Many of the Hunter's Choice crowd probably would have shot either the doe or the earlier fawn, though it's doubtful any of them would have hiked that far off the road. However, I hadn't passed up bucks I had seen earlier, including a forked-horn and a three-point as recently as two days earlier, so that I could shoot a doe. I was holding out for a big old boy.

By the fast, deliberate pace the doe was walking, I was sure a buck was on her trail. As soon as the doe disappeared down the trail to my left, I heard another limb pop to the right. You better believe I was excited and ready! Three seconds later a beautiful, majestic, multi-pointed buck—with his head held high and chin pointed toward the ground—appeared, only about forty yards behind the doe, stepping right out. When I saw his four-point rack, I knew he was mine. I shot at his left rib-cage as he passed broadside and slightly uphill from me forty yards away. He didn't react, so I aimed again. When I shot, he fell down and rolled over a couple times on the slope. Ecstatic!, I hustled up to him. He wanted to get up but couldn't. When I determined that he was not going to die immediately, I finished him with an upper neck shot. Upon looking him over, I found my first shot had hit farther back than I wanted, just behind his liver. My second bullet had shattered on a small maple limb a few feet before getting to the buck, and the main chunk had broken his upper left leg just below the shoulder but stopped short of his vitals. Numerous pieces of shrapnel had penetrated his flesh in the shoulder area, but did only superficial damage. I thanked God for again seeing fit to bless me with a big, old blacktail buck! It was 8:20 a.m. Needless to say, I was very glad I had passed on lesser bucks earlier in the

*Murphey's Funnel pays off!*

season. A hunter can never be certain he will see another buck during the season, let alone a large one, so passing one up is risky. Very few blacktail hunters that I know of take that risk.

After completing the field-dressing, I packed the big buck out the three-fourths of a mile to the road, photographed it, loaded it in my truck and then drove home to proudly show it to

Dad, who had kept my son Cody overnight. I passed Dad on his way to the dump and stopped him.

He asked, "Did you get one?"

I jumped out and said, "Yeh, I got a four-point!"

He then got out of his truck and came over to mine. Upon seeing the buck he said, "How do you do it?"

My dad is a very good fisherman and was an excellent duck hunter and a good trapper in his younger years, but never took to deer hunting like I do. He did, however, take an avid interest in and was an expert at hunting arrowheads and authored How To Find Indian Arrowheads. I only hunted deer with Dad one time, my first year home from the Navy. So when Dad sees my big bucks and asks, "How do you do it?" I can't help but feel proud and yet think of the many times over the years I have asked him the same question concerning so many other things.

I may not be successful at a lot of things, but I have found my niche when it comes to getting lucky on big blacktail bucks. I knew that sooner or later, my streak of luck would again end, but at least I had another ten and a half months after the 1992 season to savor the latest reward for my perseverance afield.

*He shouldn't have followed that doe.*

# FALL 1993
# A HUNTER'S RAMBLINGS

The writeup of this season has been done in diary form, though it has been edited to not include every entry during the 1993 deer season.

SEPT 29th- Deer season is only three days away, and my anticipation is becoming almost unbearable. Yesterday I sighted-in my rifle (usually I don't wait until the last minute like this). After fine tuning my 30.06, I was joined by my sister Colleen, a deputy sheriff in Nebraska who was on vacation to Oregon, in shooting over 300 rounds of ammo through my .22 carbine and .22 revolver. We had a great time. Unfortunately, that activity cost me three hours of sleep during the night as I awakened and then couldn't keep my mind off deer hunting.

I've been out scouting only a few times—in the brush once—because of my full-time responsibilities with my two young children. While scouting, I saw plenty of deer sign in every area I checked, confirming that the blacktail populations in those areas are doing well. Regrettably, I also found that a mobile home has been moved into the bottom side of Clearcut B below Murphey's Funnel. That will undoubtedly have undesirable effects on the deer activity there.

Hunting conditions are very poor because we've had only a trace of rain for the whole month of September here in the upper Willamette Valley. This season I'm going to break my pattern of hunting solo by getting out with a few friends on some hunts. My goal is to shoot a four-point or better buck, though I'd consider taking a very nice three-point.

OCT 2nd- Opening day. Hot and dry, temps into mid-80's by mid-afternoon. Full moon last night. Hooked up with Tim Watson and Dan Morgan, another Campus Crusade For Christ staffer, to hunt a six year old clearcut—I'll call this "Clearcut D" and label the surrounding area "Berryhill"—on the north side of Lookout Point Reservoir.   Clearcut D is bordered by large Douglas fir and grand fir to the north and east, and by an older clearcut to the west.  The older clearcut is the same one where my brother Rob killed his three-point in 1984.  Of course, now it is grown up and extremely dense.  I'll confess that I didn't scout Clearcut D before the season, so I wasn't sure what to expect. I knew the lay of the land, however, from past hunting expeditions there.

The only action we had was in the morning at first light, when Tim and I jumped a deer which gave us only a brief glimpse of its rear, just after we had split off from Dan.  Tim later got another brief glimpse of what he believed was the same deer.

Deer and elk have both been browsing heavily in the unit, as it seemed that the end of every blackberry vine had been eaten.  Bear and coyote droppings abounded as well, indicating their affinity for the area.

We finished our morning hunt before 10 o'clock, at which time Dan had to leave to meet another commitment.   Tim wanted to drive around to look over some other potential hunting spots, so that's what we did until mid-afteroon when we called it a day.

Tim shared an interesting acrostic he refers to when looking for deer: "'SCAM' stands for Shape, Color, Angle and Motion."  If one adds his senses of hearing (Sounds) and (Smell) to his sense of sight, he gets SCAMSS.  The attentive hunter will constantly analyze the woods environment for discrepancies in these six areas.  If something doesn't fit, the hunter must figure out why.   For example, trees grow vertically, so if a hunter sees something a couple feet off the ground that looks like part of a tree trunk lying horizontally, he better take a closer look. The Angle is wrong.  It may be a deer.  Another example would be a limb that pops.  That Sound may have been a deer stepping on a small, leaf-covered maple-branch.  **Pay Attention To Your Senses**!

OCT 4th- Monday. Hot and dry. Got out for last two hours to Berryhill- Lookout Point Reservoir, north shore. I'm having to use my hunting time to scout. Fortunately, I like what I'm finding. Still haven't gotten into the timber yet. No deer sighted. No problem.

OCT 7th- My best friend, Jesse Chapman, arrived in early afteroon with a forky mulie he shot opening day, Oct 2nd, in Central Oregon. Last year's severe and long winter in Central and Eastern Oregon took a substantial toll on the mule deer population; hardest hit were the fawns including many that would have been legal bucks this fall. As a result, the ODFW drastically reduced from last year's allotment the number of controlled mule deer tags issued. Oregon's mule deer population had been making a fairly good comeback over the previous several years thanks to mild winters and the shift from a general open season for all of Eastern Oregon to controlled entry seasons for each specific section in that part of the state east of the Cascade Mountain's summit beginning with the 1991 deer season. By going to the controlled hunt system, the ODFW controls hunter numbers in any given section thereby preventing an overkill of deer in any one area. Another benefit of the controlled entry system is that it prevents overcrowding by hunters in any one location, making for a more enjoyable hunt for those who do gain entry.

Because of last winter's devastating effects on the mule deer population, many hunters (including some of my friends) exchanged the Eastern deer tags they had drawn for Western Oregon tags. Some hunters feel that the ODFW should have cancelled all mule deer seasons this year to allow for a better carryover of deer into next year. Some have speculated that seasons were left open because if the ODFW had cancelled mule deer seasons entirely, they would have lost too much revenue from those hunters choosing to sit out the season rather than hunt blacktails in the West. The ODFW, however, said that potential lost revenue was not a factor in its decision.

Jesse said very few people were getting deer, so he had no regrets about settling for a forked-horn opening day. He had already boned out his deer's meat prior to arriving at my place, so we finished cutting it up. Then for supper, Jesse, I, and the kids had a feast of fried mule deer steak, french fries and my home canned pickles. Many times in the past Jesse and I had similar bachelor banquets together with anything from bear or beaver meat to deer or elk meat.

OCT 8th. Before daybreak Jesse accompanied me to Berryhill on the north side of Lookout Point Reservoir. Weather continues dry, though we had a brief shower two days ago. Temps are a little cooler, in 70's. Though we didn't see any deer in the morning hunt, I did make myself a nice blind at the base of a large grand fir tree and under some vine maple branches, overlooking a couple of good game trails leading from a steep, brushy hillside to Clearcut D. Because of the amount of elk sign in the area, I am tempted to get an elk tag to hunt during the Cascade Elk Season. We'll see.

OCT 9th- Saturday, dry-mild temps. Tim, Dan and I drove out to the Siuslaw Unit before daylight to hunt an area I knew and that I felt would be productive for the three of us working as a team. Unfortunately the gate was locked, so we crossed the freeway to hunt the Indigo Unit throughout the day. Conditions were very dry again. Actually we spent very little time in the timber—my favorite choice—for various reasons. I had a good time in their company. They're great guys who have both had many outdoor experiences including remote pack-trips and, in Tim's case, hunts. Both have hunted upland birds and squirrels extensively, something I've done very little of. Tim is quite a story teller, introducing many of his tales with, "Wes, did I ever tell you about the time...?"

At lunch time in late morning, we enjoyed a good time of swapping hunting and packing stories. Tim had talked so highly to Dan of my blacktail hunting prowess earlier—for example, when Tim and Dan had arrived at my house opening morning and Dan saw my antler collection, he asked, "Did you kill these deer in clearcuts or in the brush?" Tim had told him, "This guy hunts the brush, and I mean the heavy brush!"—that when we were exchanging hunting stories, Dan asked me, "So how close do you actually kill most your deer from anyway, Wes?"

Seeing a good opening, I answered, "Well Dan, I'm so close to most of them that I don't even use my gun, I kill 'em with my hunting knife." At least I've got a few people fooled into thinking I'm a fairly good blacktail hunter. Compared to some bow hunters, though, I'm sure I couldn't hold a candle.

I must confess that I got so caught up in our "bull session" that when we left the truck I forgot to load my weapon, and I even left my clip in the truck. We were over a half a mile from the truck in some timber when I realized what I'd done. Instead of returning to get my clip, I opted to just go ahead and chamber a round and hunt as if my auto-loader .06 was a single shot. Maybe Dan will figure out that the real reason I have to kill my deer with my hunting knife is because I'm so absent minded that I often forget to load my weapon before going on a hunt. Honestly, I have never done that before. I have, however, left home to hunt without my rifle being in my vehicle.

It's funny, a week earlier Tim had asked me, "How many deer have you killed after cleanly missing with the first shot?"

I had responded, "I've only killed one after missing with the first shot, and that was a four-point in a clearcut [1988]. I've never had that happen in the timber. So often in the timber, one shot is all you get, and you have to make it count."

I got my chance today to demonstrate my confidence that a blacktail hunter could get by with a single-shot rifle when hunting in the timber. I must admit that knowing one has a follow-up round available is comforting. As it turned out, I didn't see anything to shoot at in the next two hours before returning to the truck. At least I impressed Dan with my preparedness.

In the evening we crossed over Interstate 5 to hunt the History Hole in the Siuslaw Unit for the last hour or so of daylight. We ended the day not seeing any deer again, though Tim heard some around his dusk-time stand.

OCT 11th- Monday. Went to Berryhill to sit in my blind stand for the last hour of daylight. After hiking in three quarters of a mile to the top of Clearcut D bordering the timber where my stand was, I heard some noise just inside the timberline. Suspecting it was done by elk, I sneaked to the edge of the black-berry vines and peeked over the top in the direction of the noise. Sure enough, I spotted some elk just inside the timber. After having my sights on the kill zone of two different bulls—a spike and a forked-horn—at a distance of seventy yards, I made up my mind to sneak back down the mountain and forego the deer hunting for the day. I plan to be up at Berryhill at day-light Saturday morning in hopes of catching the elk there. I'll stay out of the area for the rest of the week.

OCT 12th- Tues. Drove out to Bell Road in the Siuslaw Unit to hunt the last two hours of day. Was extremely disappointed to find a brand new—built within previous month—logging spur road going through the middle of the second-growth timber on the top of Billy Butte. Talk about spoil my enthusiasm. Over the past six years, I've really enjoyed hunting that small moun-tain. Besides the one new spur road, I found two other new spurs going out to the tops of the other two small mountains off Bell Road's north fork. Unfortunately, my second choice hunt-ing area on Bell Road's south fork is being logged off right now. I don't mean to get on a bandwagon, but I've gotten the im-pression over the last three years that there is a race going on in the Beaver Creek Valley, particularly on Bell Road, to see who can log their lands off first. Certainly clearcutting lots of large timber is a boon to the blacktail population, but finding large tracts of big timber to hunt in is becoming harder and harder in Lane County. Of course, I realize that timber is not managed for the benefit of a deer hunter like me.

OCT 16-22. I didn't do any deer hunting this week as I got a Cascade Elk tag. I was pretty naive to think I might have a herd of elk to myself. Several other hunters worked Berryhill and the surrounding area also. Due to the childcare situation, I was only able to get out for two full days and one other evening. Until my circumstances change, I'd best forget elk hunting be-cause I get too frustrated at my limited opportunities to hunt. While hunting the elk, I got on to some fresh sign, but the elk had already been run out by other hunters.

OCT 23rd- Saturday. Weather dry and mild. Still-hunting conditions are poor. Hunted all day off north fork of Bell Road. Jumped a young buck in late afternoon—I think it was only a forked-horn—from its bed in a vine-maple thicket twenty-five yards downhill to my right while hunting a timbered area thick with vine maple. I'll call this area "Maylet Valley." Earlier in the day while hunting Hawk's Butte (the next hill to the north of Billy Butte, an area I've hunted before) on the south side of Maylet Valley I winded deer downhill from me on the west side of the hill. However, with the dried oak and madrone leaves all over and heavy brush, I opted not to attempt to move in on the deer downhill in their beds. While walking the gravel road up to the truck around three p.m. between hunts, I saw a big coyote run across the road about forty yards ahead of me. I've seen them in the timber while hunting in this area before. Took a stand for last hour and a half without any luck. I found the lower half of a large antler early in the day.

OCT 24th- Got out for afternoon-evening hunt. Saw nothing except a doe on Bell Road while driving out after dark. I spent the whole time scouting and learning the area to the north of Maylet Valley. Looks promising. At the top of Maylet Valley I found an opening between the two timbered sides of the hill that was over 300 yards long and about fifty feet wide—a grassed over dirt logging spur that had been cleared for a road but not finished several years earlier. I know that this spot would be an ideal ambush point during the rut and at other times for a hunter who wanted to sit for an extended time watching the opening between second growth fir lots. However, I am not going to be that hunter because simply killing a buck is not my objective. I want the circumstances to be desirable to me. Sitting or standing and watching this type of opening does not appeal to me. This same logic is why I won't shoot an animal I spot from my vehicle or even while walking a road (even if I get legally off the road first). Additionally, I would much rather kill a buck in the timber than in a clearcut. I guess I'm strange, but even packing my buck out is a necessary ingredient to my personal fulfilment on a successful hunt.

My personal expectations and hunting philosophy grow with each year that passes. I hope my own views and expectations never cause another hunter to be intimidated around me or to feel ashamed because his buck is "only a spike or forked-horn," or because he shot a doe or a fawn. As long as he took his game legally, I'll gladly share in his excitement.

OCT 26th- Continues warm, low 70's, and dry. Out for afternoon-evening in new area north of MV. Plenty of sign, but no deer. We need rain. Saw a doe, fawn, and black bear cub on north fork of Bell Road on way out after dark.

Oct 27th- Up to Lookout Point Blind #2 for last hour of daylight. (I made this blind on one of the afternoons I was elk hunting) Wind favorable out of the north. Still dry and warm days. Full moon. No deer sighted, though I stayed until twenty minutes after dark. I admit I'm a novice when it comes to evening stands.

OCT 30th- Saturday. To north fork Bell Road. Hiked into back clearcut to the southwest of Hawk's Butte before daylight. Nothing there; some fog problems. Then I worked the southwest and west sides of the Butte. I found one of the biggest concentrations of deer beds I've ever found, over a dozen in an area less than twenty-five yards square. Several of the beds were used a day ago. While working the west side of Hawk's Butte, I jumped a deer that I didn't get a look at. Forty-five minutes later, while working up the north side of Maylet Valley just across the way, I jumped a nice forked-horn and had him dead to rights at a distance of thirty yards, but I let him go. I want a big rack. Passing up a legal blacktail buck when one has the opportunity to bag one can come back to haunt a Western Oregon rifle hunter because opportunities generally are limited. Certainly the dry conditions this year have been a big factor in my own poor luck as far as numbers of deer seen goes. Another reason for my few sightings has been the amount of time I've spent scouting instead of hunting. I'm still enjoying the hunts though.

*A handsome forked-horn (ODFW Photo)*

NOV 5th- Friday. A cool, foggy morning. Up to Billy Butte before dawn. We finally had a real good shower two mornings ago. I parked the car over half a mile down the hill from where I entered the timber through a narrow clearcut bordering the road. I wanted to get deep enough into the timber at daylight that my form would not be backed by the clearing's light. Advancing slowly in the old growth timber at the edge of the clearing (this is the same general area where I killed the spike two years ago and an area where I've often seen deer, especially late in the day when it has rained), I spotted a fawn moving to my right about fifty yards away at 6:45. (I should mention that I had drawn an antlerless/spike permit for this area and was hoping to fill it this morning.) The wind was in my favor. Immediately, I eased my safety off, readied my rifle, and looked for other deer near the fawn. Unfortunately, several big trees blocked my view. As soon as the fawn moved out of sight, I sneaked in closer, keeping a lookout for deer anywhere ahead of me and to my sides.

This is always a ticklish predicament because if even one deer spots the hunter first, the other deer will get alerted immediately by the first deer's body language—stiffening up and becoming alert, motionless, and with ears out and head up facing the area of concern. Once that happens, the hunter's chances for a good shot on the deer of his choice become very slim, particularly when all the sight lanes between trees are only inches wide. The very thing that allows a hunter to get in close to deer in big timber without seeing them or being seen himself—the size of the trees and their close proximity—could cost him a deer if he is spotted before seeing his target.

Two minutes later, after moving forward ten more yards, I spotted what I believed was a doe move to the right of some trees ahead about forty yards and to the right of me. I was standing next to a big fir tree, so I used it to lean my rifle against in readying for a shot. I wanted either a doe, spike or a large-antlered buck. I definitely did not want to shoot a fawn or a forked-horn. If I shot a forked-horn, I would have to use my general buck tag on it, which I was saving for a big buck. The early morning low-light conditions made it hard to be sure the adult-sized deer didn't have antlers. I cranked my scope up to about seven power and found I couldn't see the deer at all because of the lighting and shade around the deer. By then I got the shakes and managed to breath into my scope while turning it down to four power. At once, I wiped the fog off the lens with a tissue from my front shirt pocket, and took a couple deep breaths to get control of myself. At any moment the broadside deer, which was munching on grass and ferns, would move out of the narrow sightline forcing me to decide on my next strategy. The deer's head at that moment was out of my sight behind a tree to the right. Then the deer turned and took a few steps directly away from me. I was fairly sure it was a doe from the quick glimpses I'd had at its head. Still I waited. Determining body size and antler status can be difficult in low light situations, and I needed to be certain. Finally, the deer turned around completely and I got a positive ID. It was a doe. It turned a little to its left and gave me a front angled shot at its right rib cage just behind the leg. "Boom!" She went right down as at least one other deer ran into the heavy brush to the right of her. My bullet hit her right lung, liver, and paunch, exiting out the left side. She was dead in seconds. Had I been thinking, I would have waited to move in to gut the deer out in case any other deer crossed through the area at that time of morning.

While bent down over the deer to gut it, I noticed an antlerless deer move to my left thirty yards away near the clearing from the direction I had just come. My rifle was lying five feet away, so I slowly retrieved it in case a large-antlered buck was with the other deer. Immediately, I spotted a second doe to the right of the first deer; it was frozen and looking right at me. In a few seconds they both turned and ran off. They had come from the same area I had passed through fifteen minutes earlier. Two minutes later, while foolishly continuing the gutting process, I heard crunching behind me from the thick brush where the deer had run at the sound of my shot. I quickly grabbed my gun, which was now lying next to me and turned to look behind me. Two fawns, standing fifteen yards away, were shocked to see me and ran off at once. Had either been the buck I was after I would have had a good shot. At that point I should have quit working on the doe and got into position for any other deer that might be moving through. I didn't. Three minutes later there was some loud crashing close behind me and I quickly grabbed my rifle and turned my head to look. My quick movements alerted the big buck twenty yards away, which instantly bolted out of sight behind some big trees. I saw at least three points, though its rack was not exceptional or as large as some of my recent ones. Honestly, I'm not certain I would have taken it if I could have. After the buck disappeared in the timber, I heard a deer blow from the buck's general direction. I don't know if it was the buck or not.

After completing the field dressing, I hid the doe and continued my hunt eventually ending up down at Murphey's Funnel for the first time all year. From Stand Two on the hillside I could see the new mobile home 300 yards below me in Clearcut B. So much for the serenity I enjoyed here in the past. The new dirt logging spur above comes to within a couple hundred yards of my stand also. I sat there from ten until noon without any luck. After that I hiked out to the road below and returned to the top of Billy Butte to retrieve the doe. I found a very small forked antler on Billy Butte.

NOV 6th- Saturday. Opening day of Hunter's Choice. I hiked into my blind above Berryhill at Lookout Point Reservoir at daylight, but due to terribly dry conditions and an overabundance of maple leaves, branches, and twigs, I made a lot of noise on my way in. No deer came through in sight of my blind in the two hours I was there before heading home for the day.

NOV 7th- Took a stand in late afternoon in my blind at Hawk's Butte, but saw no deer. The new logging road to the top of the butte has totally disrupted the deer's activities there. I could hear several vehicles drive in and out above me and even heard some hunters talking. If I were a deer, I would avoid the area too.

NOV 8th- Monday. I hiked into Maylet Valley area before dawn. An hour after daylight I spotted a doe moving along uphill from me about forty yards. Behind her was a young buck which looked to be a small three-point. Maple branches were pretty thick partially obscuring my view. The doe happened to look my way and immediately became alert and moved to get out of sight of me. Had I been inclined to, I could have shot the young buck while his body was clearly exposed to me, but he was not big enough for what I wanted, so I didn't squeeze. He followed the doe in her careful escape back up the hill out of my sight.

Half an hour later, while looking down a narrow sight lane below me on the steep hill with fairly dense fir and maple trees,

I spotted a doe moving slowly along toward the sight lane from the left. I was hoping a buck would be on her tail—as the rut was in full swing—but that was not the case. I watched her until she disappeared in the brush to the right five minutes later.

Over an hour later, at around ten o'clock, as I was sitting watching a likely area below me, I had a doe and a forked-horn pass by broadside to me fifteen feet away as they headed uphill by way of the crease coming up out of the valley floor. The little fork was right on her tail. They didn't even notice me. She was too busy playing hard to get, and he was determined not to be denied. I easily could have shot him, but passed.

About an hour and a half after seeing the last young buck, I walked through the opening at the top of Maylet Valley that I described on Oct. 24th. While there I found a small, fresh gut pile from a buck. I knew it was a buck because its genital organs were left. Interestingly, the lungs were not present, but I'm not sure why. I've heard that some hunters eat deer lungs. Obviously some hunter had taken advantage of this opening and been successful as I had anticipated. Maybe he shot one of the two young bucks I passed on earlier in the morning? I hunted two more hours and then quit for the day.

NOV 9th- Tuesday. Hunted all day around Billy Butte area. Saw three deer at close range from my stand at last light, but not the big buck I wanted.

NOV 10th- Wednesday. Final day of regular season. Unable to get out until noon. Went to History Hole in Siuslaw Unit for first time all year except for last hour opening day. Spotted a bedded doe under some hazel nut branches across a draw seventy-five yards away. I watched her for over five minutes while making various noises to see if I could get her or any other deer which I couldn't see to move. Finally, she tired of my games and she and another doe nearby sneaked out the back of their hiding spot. I could have shot either one. I drove back to Bell Road area to sit at Murphey's Funnel for last hour. But no luck. Now all I can do is go back out to the Willamette Unit to hunt for the first time since 1986. This time, however, I'm going there because I chose to pass up some small legal bucks, not because I didn't get a shot at one.

NOV 12th- Friday. Took kids and drove out to the Willamette Unit west of Eugene to see about gaining access to some private property. Secured permission to hunt Gibson's (hereon known as Fir Song Acres—earlier described), as well as a much larger piece to the north that I will call Nell's Ranch. While at Nell's ranch I got to see a wide, high, and very heavy-antlered four-point buck's head that the owner had shot the night before while the buck chased a doe in their yard between apple trees at last light. What a trophy! It may even make the record book. In talking to a neighbor a few miles to the northwest, I learned that a four-point and five-point were taken earlier in the season near that edge of Nell's Ranch. At least I know there are some good genetics in the area.

NOV l4th- Got out to Nell's Ranch by 2:30 p.m. Entered from southwest access point and used most of my time to scout, since I've never been on the property before. The owners have selectively logged much of the various hill's south slopes in the last year with the use of cats. The skid roads, trails, and all the leftover debris definitely make still-hunting much of the timber unrealistic. Visibility is blocked by brush, and the branches lying all about the ground make being quiet impossible. After hiking into the northeast over a mile on a dirt cat road, I got into an area I feel will be more suited to my hunting style. I scared a heavy deer in some thick brush downhill from the cat road at one point. I'm sure it was a big buck.

NOV 18th- Thursday. Very foggy after rain last two days. At Fir Song Acres before dawn. The day was unfruitful as far as deer sightings—only saw one briefly. During the day I covered a lot of ground in order to scout, and learned how much things have changed since the last year I hunted here (1986). So much of the area has been logged that I hardly knew it. In a few years, Seneca's huge clearcut adjoining this piece will prove to be a boon to the local deer population. There are plenty of deer using the west and southsides of the property now, but much of the brush there is very heavy. Additionally, the deer can seek sanctuary on the adjoining properties which I do not have access to. Some houses have gone up around the east and north perimeters of the property, further restricting my hunting. One thing I'm coming to realize as of this year is that I'm going to have to learn to be an effective stand hunter—whether I want to or not—because of how many fewer big timber stands there are available in the local area than in years past. It only takes one year to remove a stand of big timber, but it takes a good forty before it even begins to resemble the same forest it was before being cut. In most cases it takes much longer. I won't live that long.

NOV 20th- Saturday. Into Nell's Ranch from southwest before daylight. Fog was very thick. Unfortunately, I took the wrong cat road in the morning fog and darkness and didn't get to my first light destination until two hours after dawn. I did jump two heavy deer, getting a quick look at one big buck. The foggy conditions really worked against me.

Around noon, while working through a timbered area on a north slope, I spotted a red fox ahead of me, moving along toward me as it sniffed the ground. I stepped behind a large fir tree and watched as the fox came within twelve feet of me. At that distance it happened to look my way and, though I was perfectly still, the fox knew I didn't belong and it immediately dashed away to a safer distance—about thirty-five yards—before resuming its ground sniffing activities.

NOV 21st- Sunday afternoon. To Fir Song Acres for last three hours. First time all season I've gotten to hunt in the rain—very unusual for Oregon. No deer. Found good sign and several fresh buck rubs.

NOV 24th- Nell's Ranch. Snow to four inches deep on most of ground. Hard frozen surface due to fifteen degree temps. last night. The only way to hunt these conditions is on stand. Took the opportunity to walk out more of the land. I have to admit that I am beginning to get discouraged about my chances for a big buck.

NOV 25th- Happy Thanksgiving! I thank God for my two children and for all the other positive people in my life. When I'm at home, I don't feel very positive about my chances for my buck, but when I'm in the brush, I am still very optimistic.

NOV 27th- Saturday. Freezing rain. My friend Mark Adkins, a Eugene area private contractor, followed me out to Nell's Ranch and walked in with me, splitting off and taking a right fork to the area to the east of where I hunted. The freezing rain made for treacherous walking. Anybody with half a lick of sense wouldn't have bothered. Combined with the snow remaining on the ground, still-hunting conditions were pathetic except in isolated pockets. While hunting through such a pocket at about 10 a.m., I found the remains of a very nice four-point buck only a few days old. Coyotes had eaten all the hide and flesh from the skeleton, and even chewed up the small bones. There was only a few inches of the rib bones left. I looked for skeletal damage but found none. Though I couldn't be certain, I guessed that the deer had been wounded by a hunter's bullet and then not recovered. Whether the coyotes found it after it had died or brought it down after it was weak, I don't know. I cut the skull off and hung it up in a tree and returned after dark to retrieve it. Finding the buck only reinforced my resolve to shoot only a big buck.

An hour later, at about 11 o'clock, I spotted a deer to my right about seventy-five yards away moving to the left. Because of the heavy brush I lost sight of it at once. The hard crunchy ground made stalking impossible, so I moved ahead just enough to put myself in position to maybe see the deer if it continued for some distance to its left. It did, as I got a good opportunity on it ten minutes later. Unfortunately, it was a doe. A minute later another deer, which I was almost sure I saw small antlers on, crossed through behind the first deer. Had I seen a big rack, I would have dropped it. I followed out in the direction they were working without seeing them again or any other deer.

In talking to Mark tonight, he said he only hunted the first hour or so and didn't see any deer. He was impressed with all the coyote tracks in the snow though, just as I was.

NOV 28th- Sunday. Warmer, into forties. To Fir Song Acres for last two and a half hours. Nothing.

NOV 29th- Fir Song Acres all day. Very windy conditions in the afternoon, not good for deer hunting. Also dangerous to be under big trees because of falling branches. Loggers refer to such branches as "widow makers," for obvious reasons. In the morning I watched four does for over half an hour from sixty yards away in the thinned second-growth timber below the landowners' house. Actually, one of them had spotted me and alerted the others. However, I don't think the deer were sure what I was because they continued to feed intermittently while working toward heavier brush. I remained motionless, partially hidden behind trees while resting my rifle against a tree and hoping to see a buck in the bunch. No such luck. The deer eventually made their way to safety. I could have taken any of them.

NOV 30th- Last chance. Intermittent rains. Fir Song Acres again. I watched a doe cross through from a clearcut into heavy brush and hardwoods just after daylight at a distance of 125 yards. She kept looking back and I hoped she was waiting for a buck. I told Dad last night that I was going to take the first doe I saw in order to at least come away with some meat. However, when the opportunity was there, I couldn't settle for the doe. I still believed I would get a buck. As it happened, I didn't see any other deer the rest of the day. My streak of nice buck years has finally come to an end. Surprisingly, it doesn't bother me as much as I thought it would, I think partly because I have come to realize that I don't have anything to prove. At any rate, I had an enjoyable season, aside from some of the new developments in the Bell Road area.

Before next year I'm going to have to get out and find some new hot spots. The logging and influx of hunters has changed everything in my areas off Bell Road.

The Oregon Department of Fish and Wildlife announced earlier in the season that beginning next season there will no longer be a Northwest Hunter's Choice Season at the end of the regular blacktail deer season. Instead, the Dept. will be issuing many more antlerless/spike permits on a drawing basis—giving more hunters the opportunity to harvest two deer though the total harvest is expected to be about the same—in the areas previously open for any deer during the Hunter's Choice seasons of the past. I'm in favor of this new move. I believe it will spread the hunting pressure out better throughout the latter part of the season instead of everyone thronging to the woods for the last five days as has been happening. It will provide additional revenue to the ODFW. And finally, it will give the ODFW the ability to directly control how many does are taken in a given year.

*Cody and Tasha Murphey in camp at*
*Crescent Lake (1993)*

# ANTLER MYSTIQUE

The fourteen year-old boy, carrying a lever action 30-30 Winchester, hiked down the opposite side of the butte from where his dad was hunting, hoping to see a buck on that warm October afternoon. When he came to a large fir log, he climbed up on top of it. Suddenly, a buck exploded from its bed next to the log. The badly shaken boy never got off a shot. Later, when he rejoined his dad, he explained ecstatically, "Dad, I scared a huge buck from next to a big log, but I didn't get off a shot! He had horns growing out from all over his head." The boy's dad had told him about many of his own past hunting experiences, and the boy had often fantasized as he looked over his dad's antler collection. No doubt the buck the boy jumped was a nice one, but "horns growing out from all over his head"?

Even an antler found lying along a deer trail will cause the imagination of many a hunter or hiker to come alive. Like the shed snake skin found next to a dead log, or the crawdad shell that is found in a stream's shallow eddy, a shed antler is a positive sign of its previous wearer's having survived another growing season or, in the case of deer, another hunting season. Contrast that to the finding of a bone or a skull indicating the animal's demise. What is it about antlers that so many hunters, and even many non-hunters, find so fascinating? Why do so many hunters expend so much time, energy, and money— many times enduring very poor weather conditions and much frustration—trying to put a set of antlers on their walls? What is this antler mystique?

Antlers are unique to the deer family which includes elk, moose, caribou, and several species and subspecies of deer. All male members of the deer species and female caribou grow antlers, though the antlers of female caribou are very small in comparison to those of the males. Deer grow their first set of antlers during the late spring and summer of their second year of life and shed them the following winter after mating season is over. They continue to regrow and then shed their antlers every year thereafter. Normally, the older a deer gets the larger its antlers grow, but this pattern can be disrupted by insufficient food or mineral consumption during the antler growing months from spring through late summer. Also a very old deer will often revert to growing diminished-sized antlers—sometimes with even a reduction in antler points—perhaps because it doesn't eat as well or because its body doesn't process its food as efficiently as it once did or because of hormonal changes.

Antlers are very similar to bone in that they grow out of blood made up of protein, calcium and other minerals which are somehow genetically programmed to grow in a certain configuration. But whereas bones are identical in form—though they vary in size and bulk—from one member of any given animal species to the other members, antlers vary greatly in configuration from one member to the next. Antlers in a given geographic area may, however, be similar in form between animals as a result of a common gene pool, but each is still unique.

During the antler-growing period the antlers are protected by a skin-like material covered with very fine, short hair which resembles velvet. Thus the phrase "in the velvet" is used to describe the growing antlers. Antlers are very durable once hardened, but they are easily damaged by contact while in the velvet stage. Often an antler that was damaged while growing will have a big knot at the injury site and have other deformities, such as an oversized eye guard (or brow tine) or a crooked growth pattern. While deer are growing their antlers, they generally avoid the heaviest brush where damage to the developing antlers can occur.

In late summer, when the antlers are fully developed, deer use trees to rub off the now dead and dry velvet skin covering their antlers. Then the male deer will fight each other by knocking their antlers together and having pushing and shoving matches to establish their dominance or pecking order. The strongest males will have first "breeding rights" once the females come into estrous, ready to be bred. Often dominance among males is established on the basis of antler size or body size alone and no actual fighting occurs. Aside from their use as weapons for determining dominance, the antlers also serve as sexual ornaments.

Throughout history antlers have been used by men for numerous purposes. For example, American Indians used them for pressure flaking small stones in the fabrication of arrowheads, and also for jewelry, among other things. The American frontiersmen used antlers for knife handles. Today there is a great market for antlers in some oriental countries where they are said to be used in soups and other foods for medicinal and aphrodisiacal purposes. Though I question the actual value of antlers as an aphrodisiac, I believe the reason they may be considered such is because many people see antlers as the symbol of a male deer's majesty, its power, its virility, and its masculinity. Antlers are, in fact, directly linked to a male deer's sexual instincts in that they are used in determining dominance among males, and they are fully mature and usable for only a portion of the year, that part coinciding with the deer's breeding season.

Antlers are also used in many art forms including being mounted as a set, either on wood plaques or as part of a head mount. Like other types of art, the beauty found in any given set of antlers is seen through "the eyes of the beholder." One person is most impressed by very large typically-shaped antlers, while someone else is more interested in a smaller non-typical (or oddly shaped) set. At the 1992 Blacktail Hunter's Convention in Eugene, Oregon, I thoroughly enjoyed looking at all of the trophy mounts displayed. There were many large bucks, including some record book bucks, exhibited. The head mount that I found to be the most beautiful, however, was a blacktail spike-buck with artificial snow on its head and nose.

I personally have never had any of my deer heads mounted for a few reasons—two being lack of space for displaying and the cost to do so. I have, however, mounted many of my antlers as sets on wood plaques, and I have mounted them for numerous other people. Certainly a set of mounted antlers takes up considerably less room-space than a full head

*Wes with his three-point or better blacktail racks taken between 1979 and 1993. (He killed all but the four-point in the middle which he found in 1993.)*

and shoulder mount. I find a nicely mounted set of antlers alone to be a beautiful piece of artwork.

Besides their beauty as art, antlers also serve to be a tangible reminder—and in some crowds, necessary evidence—of a particular hunting experience. When I look at the antlers from any of the deer I've killed, I can drift back in time to that day's hunt and relive the experience, even feeling some of the emotions I felt on that successful hunt. Each set is unique and has its own story.

Although I have mentioned several ways in which antlers are used and in which they captivate the interest or imagination of various people, I think for me the thing that demonstrates the antler mystique the most is the effect they can have on a hunter when he sees them on a deer during the open hunting season.

Seeing a set of antlers on a buck can turn the calmest, most reserved individual into an excited nervous wreck, with a terrible case of the shakes, in a split-second. A veteran shooter, who can hit a quarter consistently with his rifle at a distance of 100 yards, can be so shaken up at having a buck jump up from its bed a few yards away that he can't even think to take his safety off. Then when he does, he cleanly misses the deer running broadside to him at less than twenty-five yards. Finally, after the buck is gone and the woods return to quiet, he curses himself while wondering why he had been so critical of other hunters' shooting ability when they told him of opportunities they had missed to bag a buck and hang its antlers on their walls because they had fallen prey to "buck fever." At times like this a hunter will swear that the deer's antlers seemed to have some kind of power over him, a power that he can't explain.

Perhaps antlers do have an unexplainable power. Maybe the oriental people are right. Certainly antlers have the power to captivate the interest and imagination of millions of hunters. Yes, maybe it is that power that is the antlers' mystique.

# HUNTING ACCIDENTS

As a hunter I have often wondered how many people actually are shot while pursuing their hunting activities. I have also wondered what the exact causes of any accidents were. My curiosity finally led me to write to Oregon's Department of Fish and Wildlife in the spring of 1993 to secure its data on hunting accidents involving firearms for the five-year period from 1988-1992. Additionally, I wanted to find out if most of the accidents that did occur would have been prevented by the victims' wearing of blaze-orange colored clothing as has been speculated by some people who propose the mandated wearing of blaze-orange colored clothing by all hunters.

The ODFW sent me a computer printout containing the following specific data for each hunting-related firearms-accident for the period requested: type of weapon used (e.g. handgun, rifle, shotgun, bow); the weapon's calibre, make, and model; type of game hunted; whether the victim was wearing blaze-orange colored clothing if it was a two-party accident; the outcome of the shooting (fatal or non-fatal); whether the shooting was self-inflicted or two-party; cause of accident; age of the shooter; whether the accident was vision related (e.g. victim out of sight of shooter or victim mistaken for game); whether the shooter was a Hunter's Safety Course graduate; whether the accident involved a law violation; and, finally, in some cases, some comment about the accident.

I compiled various statistics from the ODFW's printout to see if there were any specific patterns to or reasons for the accidents. Because I know statistics can become tedious and boring, I have tried to limit my use of them. However, I did want to bring out some of the specific numbers I discovered. To be honest—probably because I have always had a fascination with numbers and statistics (I was a statistician for some of the varsity and junior varsity athletics teams throughout my years in high school, and I used numbers constantly in submarine navigation while in the Navy.) I found the information supplied by the ODFW to be very interesting. I must admit, though, that the raw statistics here—as with almost every other use of statistics—do not tell the whole story. For example, the ODFW printout for 1988-1992 did not mention other factors that may have contributed to some of the accidents—such as weather conditions (rain or fog), time of day (lowlight of dawn or dusk), possible sun-glare, etc. However, in addition to the data from the ODFW, I received a summary of the hunting accidents that occurred in Oregon in 1992 (minus one accident) from the Oregon Sportsmen's Defense Fund. (OSDF is a non-profit, united sportsmen's group protecting the heritage and rights of Oregon's sportsmen.) I have included OSDF's whole summary as I believe it is of interest to all hunters and outdoorsmen.

I realize that the data discussed here represents only the hunting-related firearms accidents that occurred in Oregon during the five-year period from 1988-1992 and may not reflect accurately on accidents that occurred in any or all other states during the named time period. The accident rate or the cause of accidents may be quite different in those states with much more open country than is typical in over a third of Oregon. Other factors which could bear on other states' accident rates are density of hunters in a given area at a given time within a state, how much hunting is done in snowy or inclement weather, ages of hunters in a particular area, whether or not—with the antlered species—a "Hunter's Choice" season is allowed (a hunter that must identify antlers is probably more likely to wait for positive identification of his target before pulling the trigger), whether a state mandates hunters to wear blaze-orange clothing or not, and many other factors.

To begin, here is the Hunting Accident Summary 1992, courtesy of the Oregon Sportsmen's Defense Fund:

## TWO PARTY ACCIDENTS

### Mistaken For Game

**92-1** The victim was shot in the chest with a .243 by his 12-year-old grandson who thought he was shooting at a deer. It was a foggy, overcast morning and the victim was not wearing blaze-orange. The distance between victim and shooter was about 100 yards. The shooter graduated from Hunter Education in 1992. FATAL

**92-2** The 18-year-old victim, who was a Hunter Education graduate, was shot with a 30.06 at last light by a woodcutter who thought he was shooting at a deer. The victim was not wearing blaze-orange. The shooter fired from a vehicle and has been charged with manslaughter. FATAL

**92-3** The victim was sitting above a clearcut at dawn when she was shot by another hunter with a 7mm magnum, who was about 100 yards below her. Victim was not wearing blaze-orange. The shooter has been charged with manslaughter. FATAL

**92-4** The victim, dressed in camo clothing, was bow hunting, with the landowner's permission, on land owned by the shooter and was mistaken for a bear at a range of 31 yards. The shooter, using a .250 Savage, was hunting without a tag and has been charged with manslaughter. FATAL

**92-5** The victim was mistaken for an elk and was shot with a 30.06 Remington by a member of his hunting party. Both had taken Hunter Education many years ago, but neither were wearing blaze-orange or any other distinctive clothing. FATAL

**92-6** The victim, a 16-year-old Hunter Education graduate, who was dressed in drab colored clothing, was shot by an unknown hunter who apparently mistook him for a deer. Two shots were fired, the first hit the ground by his feet and when he started running, he was shot in the knee. The shots were fired from at least 400 yards away. NOT FATAL

**92-7** The victim and the shooter were members of the same eight-person deer-hunting group that was "driving" a clearcut in the Coast Range. The shooter was on a stand and the victim, who was wearing a grey sweatshirt, was one of the "drivers." He was mistaken for a buck at about 75 yards and was hit in the shoulder with one round from a 300 Weatherby magnum. NOT FATAL

92-8   The victim, a non-hunter, was walking her dog in a wooded area near her home when she was shot in the shoulder by a deer hunter with a .22 Remington.  She was wearing a white coat and the weather and visibility were poor.  The shooter was cited.  NOT FATAL

### Victim Out Of Sight Of Shooter
92-9   The shooter and his grandson shot uphill at a deer.  They heard yelling and found that their bullets had hit a pickup truck and slightly injured the driver and passenger on a road above.  They could not see the truck because of fog, and said that they did not even know there was a road above them.  NOT FATAL

### Bird Hunting Accident
92-10   The victim was hunting pheasants in a corn-stubble field with a young man who allegedly stumbled and fell, causing his shotgun to discharge.  The victim received severe injuries to the lower right leg.  NOT FATAL

### Firearms in Vehicles
92-11   The victim was in the process of giving permission to two visiting hunters for them to shoot squirrels on his property.  He asked to look at a .22 rifle in the vehicle, and as it was being passed out of the vehicle, it discharged and a round hit him in the foot.  NOT FATAL

## Self Inflicted Injuries

92-12   The passenger in a pickup truck was holding his loaded .243 bolt action Remington muzzle down.  When he saw a deer and started to exit, he pulled the trigger and shot himself in the right leg.  NOT FATAL

92-13   The passenger in a pickup truck was holding his 7mm Weatherby between him and the driver with the muzzle pointing up.  It discharged and a bullet hit him in the left arm.  NOT FATAL

### Self Inflicted Handgun Accidents
92-14   Victim was hunting rabbits with a .22 Ruger semi-automatic handgun when a "jam" occurred.  He sat on the tailgate and was in the process of clearing it when he accidentally released

the slide causing a round to discharge and pass through the soft tissue of his thigh. NOT FATAL

**92-15** Victim was assisting his partner with a wounded bear and shot himself in the leg while drawing his .357 revolver from the holster. NOT FATAL

**92-16** The victim was carrying a .45 single-action revolver with all chambers loaded while rifle hunting for deer. While making a "nature call," he slipped down a bank and the gun discharged, causing a wound to the right thigh. NOT FATAL

Carelessness With A Loaded Weapon

**92-17** The victim, a 17-year-old Hunter Education graduate, was standing with the muzzle of his .243 Browning resting on his foot. When he heard a noise and started to raise his rifle, his finger depressed the trigger and he shot himself in the foot. NOT FATAL

**92-18** A 15-year-old Hunter Education graduate slipped as she was climbing a steep hillside. She threw her .32 caliber, model 94 Winchester to one side, and it discharged. The bullet hit a rock and fragments of rock and bullet caused minor injuries to her leg. NOT FATAL

The final firearms accident for 1992, which was not included in the OSDF summary, was also a FATAL accident in which the victim was not wearing blaze-orange and was mistaken for a deer. That makes a total of six fatalities in 1992, compared to an average of 2.5 over the previous four years.

These summaries give a pretty clear picture as to what happened in each firearms accident, so I will only make a few comments. Obviously, most of these accidents could have been avoided. There is no excuse for a hunter mistaking a human for an animal. The woman who was walking her dog when shot could turn into hunters worst enemy if she decided to lump all hunters into the same class as the one that shot her. That kind of incident is the worst kind of fuel for the anti-hunter crowd to get ahold of.

Now for some numbers for the whole five year period, 1988-1992:

| DEER AND ELK HUNTERS | | | | | |
|---|---|---|---|---|---|
| | Deer Hunters | Accidents | Elk Hunters | Accidents | Deer-Elk Fatalities |
| 1988 | 259,349 | 4 | 113,718 | 2 | 1 |
| 1989 | 248,518 | 8 | 114,110 | 1 | 2 |
| 1990 | 274,281 | 12 | 110,504 | 3 | 2 |
| 1991 | 254,825 | 4 | 117,342 | 2 | 2 |
| 1992 | 247,996 | 12 | 128,560 | 2 | 5 |
| Total | 1,284,969 | 40 | 584,234 | 10 | 12* |

* Two of these fatalities were shot by hunters who were drunk mistaking them for game. Three more were self-inflicted. One other one was killed by a partner unloading his weapon in or on the vehicle. The final six fatalities were mistaken for game; five for deer, and one for an elk. (The details of five of those mistaken for game are included in the 1992 Accident Summary above.)

| ALL HUNTERS | | | | | |
|---|---|---|---|---|---|
| | Total Accidents | Fatal Accidents | Blaze-Orange Definitely Not a Factor | Self Inflicted | Vision Related |
| 1988 | 20 | 1 | 12 | 9 | 7 |
| 1989 | 27 | 4 | 15 | 10 | 10 |
| 1990 | 26 | 2 | 16 | 13 | 9 |
| 1991 | 14 | 3 | 10 | 9 | 4 |
| 1992 | 19 | 6 | 9 | 7 | 10 |
| Total* | 106 | 16 | 62 | 48 | 40 |

* These are the totals for the hunting of all game, including big game, small game, predators, water fowl, and upland birds. Note the high number of self-inflicted injuries. The total number of hunters each year averaged 336,653 not including over 80,000 permanent license holders to whom licenses have been issued in the last ten years (mostly senior citizen and pioneer licenses). [ODFW Printout 10-21-1993]

In comparing the total number of accidents to the number of deer-elk accidents, one can see that deer-elk hunters accounted for almost half of the accidents (50 of 106, forty-seven percent), yet they were responsible for three-fourths of the fatalities (12 of 16, seventy-five percent). If the three bear hunting accidents and one fatality are added in with the deer-elk, then the total number of big-game accidents and fatalities was 53 (fifty percent) and 13 (eighty-one percent). There were no accidents involving antelope and big-horned sheep hunters. The higher fatality ratio for big-game hunters—as opposed to the fatality ratio of small-game and bird hunters—can be attributed to two things: the weapon consistently involved was more powerful, and the big-game victims were mistaken for game more often, 17 times, than small-game victims, 3 times. Victims mistaken for game were consistently hit more directly.

So what weapons were involved in the 106 accidents? The breakdown is: 49 rifles, 28 handguns, 26 shotguns, 1 bow, and 2 unknown. A .22 calibre weapon was involved in the most accidents: 18 handguns, 8 rifles.

## AGE BREAKDOWN OF SHOOTER

| Age | Accidents |
|-----|-----------|
| 10-19 | 30 |
| 20-29 | 24 |
| 30-39 | 22 |
| 40-49 | 10 |
| 50-59 | 4 |
| 60 plus | 6 |
| Unknown | 10 |

Because the total number of hunters was not broken down into age groups the accident rate for each age group could not be ascertained.

How many of the 106 accidents above involved a shooter or weapon handler who was a Hunter's Safety Training graduate? Hunter's Safety graduate: 45 yes, 33 no, 28 unknown.

What were the various causes of accidents for the whole five year period, 1988-1992? (Included are the 1992 accidents summarized above.) The single biggest cause was careless handling, 28 accidents. Next, victim mistaken for game, 21 (two in which the shooter was drunk). The next five biggest causes were <u>victim out of sight of shooter</u>, 11; <u>loading or unloading weapon</u>, 9; <u>shooter stumbled</u>, 8; <u>weapon being removed from vehicle</u> 7; <u>shooter swinging his weapon</u>, 7. (Five of these were upland bird hunters swinging their shotguns, the other two were deer hunters using rifles. Surprisingly, no waterfowl hunters were shot in this manner.) Only two of these causes overlapped. The remaining accidents resulted from various other causes. Of note is the fact that 15 accidents occurred in, on, or while removing a weapon from a vehicle.

## THE BLAZE-ORANGE FACTOR

The final area I want to look at is the effect the wearing or not wearing of <u>blaze-orange</u> clothing had on the overall number of accidents. Of 106 accidents, there were 62 in which blaze-orange clothing definitely had no bearing (e.g. self-inflicted, shooter stumbled, etc.). That leaves 44. Two of those involved a drunk shooter mistaking the victims for game. That leaves 42.

Seven other victims were hit by a hunter <u>swinging his weapon</u> and firing. Interestingly, three of those <u>were wearing blaze-orange</u>, the other four were not. Twelve other victims were <u>out of sight</u> of the shooter when hit. Two of those <u>were wearing blaze-orange</u>, nine were not, and it is not known whether the other victim was wearing blaze-orange or not. Based on these 19 accidents—and their circumstances—in which 5 victims were, in fact, wearing blaze-orange, I think it would be a fair assumption to say that blaze-orange clothing probably would have made little, if any, difference in preventing the other 14 accidents had the victims been wearing it. Therefore, we can subtract another 19 from the 42 still in question above, leaving 23.

Of the final 23, nineteen were mistaken for game (one was wearing blaze-orange), and three were in the line of fire. The data on the final case was not included in the ODFW printout. Would blaze-orange clothing have prevented the 21 accidents remaining in which the victim was known to not be wearing such? It is likely that at least some of the victims would not have been shot had they been wearing blaze-orange. What we don't know in many of the final 22 accidents is what color of clothing the victims were wearing.

From the Oregon Sportsmen's Defense Fund 1992 accident summaries we do know that three of the eight victims mistaken for game (including the non-hunter woman who was walking her dog) were wearing clothing containing colors found on the big-game being hunted—definitely not advisable. Another was wearing non-distinctive clothing, while the bow hunter was wearing camoflaged clothing. We also know that the last three included in the summary were not wearing blaze-orange, but we do not know what colors they were wearing.

To put the numbers in perspective, consider that over 300,000 hunters took to the fields, woods, and waterways in each of five years for a total of well over 1.5 million hunters. Only 22 people who were shot by those hunters, in accidents where the color of clothing may have been a factor, definitely were not wearing blaze-orange clothing. Some of those were known to be wearing colors found on the game being pursued. Others were wearing non-distinctive colored clothing. The vast majority of Oregon's hunters voluntarily wear blaze-orange or other-distinctive colored clothing when hunting and did so during the five years in question. Undoubtedly more hunters would have been shot had they not been wearing some kind of distinctive-colored clothing while hunting. Certainly distinctive-colored clothing prevents accidents. Without question blaze-orange clothing is the easiest to quickly recognize under most conditions. But should all hunters—and maybe even everyone going into the woods during open hunting seasons—be required to wear blaze-orange clothing or hat wear? I don't believe so, particularly when many hunters including myself strongly believe that blaze-orange clothing is recognized by animals more easily than other distinctive colors that are popular with hunters. (Colors such as red and black plaid.)

### For the Sake of Comparison

Although each hunting accident involving a firearm is unfortunate, the hunting accident rate is actually extremely low compared to that of many other activities people take part in. Athletics is a good example. For instance, more players are injured (some severely) on any given weekend during the National Football League season—and only 28 teams of 40 plus players (a little over 1100 players) take part—than are injured by firearms during an entire year of hunting in Oregon where several hundred thousand people participate. Both football players and hunters knowingly accept whatever risks are involved when they choose to participate in their particular sports.

## CONCLUSION

Certainly the 106 accidents documented in this chapter for the period 1988-1992 in Oregon, that resulted in injury or death, do not represent the total number of incidents during that same period where a hunter was involved in a "near-miss" (or more accurately, a "near-hit"). Undoubtedly, there were other times when a weapon was discharged inadvertently but luckily didn't hit anyone. At still other times, a weapon was accidently dropped or a hunter stumbled, and yet the weapon did not fire. Guns used for target shooting or for hunting—just like many other recreational objects, or most tools when they are used— are potentially dangerous if misused or certain unpredictable circumstances occur. When people are involved in activity—be it hunting, fishing, biking, driving, athletics, horse-back riding, swimming, camping, cooking, gardening, mowing lawns, working or whatever—there will be accidents resulting in human injury and death. People make wrong decisions, they disregard safe practices, they get impatient and try to take short-cuts, etc. Without a doubt the number of firearms accidents can be held down—and has been—by Hunter's Safety Education and conscientious actions by hunters in the field.

As far as the hunting accidents that occurred in Oregon during the five-year period 1988-1992, most could, in fact, have been prevented. However, I don't believe that adopting any further regulations concerned with firearms safety will likely have much affect on the future accident rate. The only type of legislation that definitely would reduce or eliminate the number of hunting-related firearms-accidents is that which shuts down hunting entirely. That possibility is addressed in this book's final chapter—HUNTING'S FUTURE.

* In February 1994, Tony Burtt, head of the ODFW Hunter Education Program reported that hunters posted their safest year on record in Oregon during 1993 with only eight accidents, one fatality. (One other shooting fatality is under investigation and may have been hunting related.) Tragically, the fatality was a child killed when a loaded rifle in the cab of a truck accidentally discharged. Only one victim was mistaken for game. (Eugene Register Guard 2-20-94)

*(Willamette National Forest Photo)*

# HUNTING'S FUTURE

One only needs to turn on the radio or television, or scan the local newspaper to see that the future of hunting and many other outdoor pursuits is uncertain. Unfortunately, too many outdoorsmen and hunters have not gotten that message, and they think that the opportunities they now enjoy are somehow guaranteed them. These outdoorsmen take for granted that they will always be able to grab their firearms, jump in their trucks, and head out to the woods to do a little squirrel hunting, or target practicing. It's time that each outdoorsman take a good hard look at what is actually going on around him and then do his part to ensure the future he wants for himself, his children and his grandchildren is what he ends up getting.

I believe that the future of outdoor sports, particularly hunting, is dependent on three main elements. They are, nature's resources, proper wildlife management, and hunter and outdoorsmen involvement in the political process. Let's take a brief look at the part each of these elements plays in hunting's future.

## I. Nature's Resources

Nature's resources can be divided into two main types-- non-renewable (e.g. oil, precious stones and minerals) and re- newable (e.g. plants, animals, and air). Modern man in his daily living uses both of these types of resources in many cases without a thought that he could possibly use them up com- pletely or at a rate that is unsustainable over the long haul. However, there is a limit to nature's supply. "Non-renewable" means just that. Once a non-renewable resource is used up, it is gone forever. On the other hand, a renewable resource, if managed properly, will continue to exist and be renewed, thereby being available for generations to come.

So what impact does man have on nature's non-renewable and renewable resources? A good example of man's impact on a non-renewable resource is his constantly searching for a new supply of oil to tap. Man uses up one supply in one location and goes somewhere else to open up another supply. Once that supply is used up, he goes elsewhere. Someday there will no longer be a supply of oil remaining somewhere else. That will be the end of a non-renewable resource. Then the table will be turned, the non-renewable resource will be impacting man's existence.

A couple examples of man's impact on a renewable resource can be gleaned from American frontier history. Many animals were hunted or trapped at rates far exceeding the animals' ability to reproduce or renew themselves. The beaver and the buffalo are two of the most notable. While the beaver has made a tremendous comeback over the past fifty years because of good management, the buffalo exists only as a remnant of its former number because so much of its habitat was changed by the influx of people.

Today, we are seeing the negative impact that man with his constantly increasing numbers and his construction has had on numerous fish species from trout and salmon to sea-perch and bottom-fish. Here in Oregon's Willamette Valley, the streams are host to only a fraction of the fish they once harbored. I personally have seen all of the small creeks that I fished regularly as a teenager go from good fishing to very poor fishing. On some of those streams where I caught keeper fish one after another as a youth, I can fish a mile and not catch a single keeper-sized trout. Sure, a person can still catch the "planter" fish soon after they have been dumped in the stream, but the native rainbows and cutthroats are no longer there in any numbers. It breaks my heart!

Upland birds and waterfowl no longer exist in the numbers they used to here in the northwest either. Again, man's encroachment on their habitat is the primary cause.

The four things man has done that arguably have had the largest impact on wildlife and fish are: (1) build dams, (2) fill-in wetlands, (3) log old-growth timber, (4) develop on grasslands. Fortunately, most animals have adapted very well to man's intrusion into their domain and have been able to co-exist quite nicely. Many fur-bearers (including beaver, muskrat, nutria, coyote, fox, opossum, bobcat, mink and raccoon) exist in good numbers and are on the increase across much of their range. Other game animals such as deer, black bear, cougar, pronghorn and elk are also doing well throughout much of the United States. Numerous non-game species of animals are thriving today as well.

It is doubtful that many of the depleted fish numbers of various species will ever make a comeback, mainly because the water sources they live in are very vulnerable to influences such as erosion, pollution, chemical contamination, and temperature fluctuations and the human population continues to grow, thereby placing more demand on the available water supply.

By contrast, wild animals have shown they are very capable in many cases of sustaining and increasing their numbers if properly managed.

## II. Proper Wildlife Management

Proper wildlife management is accomplished when a proper balance is reached and maintained between specific animal populations, man's population, and the animals' habitat. A term frequently used in wildlife management is carrying capacity. Carrying capacity refers to a given geographical plot's ability to harbor and feed a given animal population. For example, a square mile of mixed timber-land may be able to provide a good food supply for forty deer, one bobcat, fifteen raccoons, two coyotes, various other small game, many rodents and birds. For the sake of example we will only consider the deer here. If the deer numbers are not kept in correct balance with the available food supply they will begin to take a longer-term toll on that plot's food supply. If the deer numbers go unchecked, either by man or predators, nature's management plan will go into effect. Some of the deer will leave the mile plot and move into an adjoining plot where there is more food available. At some point, however, the adjoining lands will also become overcrowded and over browsed. Then the animals' insufficient diet will result in their poorer health, poorer fawn crop, poorer fawn survival, increased vulnerability of adults and fawns to illness and disease, and finally mass die-off.

But it is not only the deer that are impacted. Often other animal species are negatively affected. At the least, the plant life is affected by being overbrowsed by the deer and may take several years or longer to recover. Allowing man, who can benefit through the use of the deer, eating its meat and using its hide, to hunt the deer to keep their numbers in proper balance with the land's carrying capacity is the most prudent way to manage the deer numbers. The same holds true for all big-game, small-game and fur-bearers. In many cases an unchecked animal population will result in the animals' becoming a nuisance and at times a hazard to people.

All animals eventually die. For man to kill an animal and eat its meat or use its fur while ensuring that its kind continues to exist and perpetuate in good numbers is proper management of one of nature's renewable resources.

### III. Hunter and Outdoorsmen Involvement in Politics

In the modern times in which we live, no man can live as an island unto himself, ignoring the political process, and still hope to have the freedoms and rights he took for granted as a youth. As hunters, outdoorsmen, gun owners and law-abiding citizens, how should we become involved in the political process?

At every opportunity we need to:

(1) Become informed on gun and outdoor issues.
(2) Vote correctly on the relevant issues.
(3) Vote for candidates who support gun-owner and hunter rights.
(4) Write letters and make phone calls to our congressman and state representatives expressing our position on the Issues.

(5) Learn about, join, and become involved in national, state and local gun-owner and outdoorsmen groups that are fighting to maintain our rights and opportunities to pursue outdoor sports and to own guns.

Probably the best way to effectively accomplish the first four items above is to begin by doing the fifth. Certainly, all groups have their shortcomings, and we can all find reasons for not belonging to or being involved with any of them. Rather than find fault, though, we should instead look at the positive things sportsmen's groups have done and continue to do. At the national level, the National Rifle Association is constantly "going to bat" on behalf of gun-owners and outdoorsmen, not to mention every law-abiding citizen. The NRA also does a good job of keeping its membership informed on gun-control issues and other anti-law-abiding-citizen agendas. On the state and local levels there are hundreds of groups all across the country that are well worth belonging to. Here in Oregon, there are many outdoor groups, from trapper and houndsmen groups to bowhunter and riflemen groups, in which outdoorsman can be involved.

In 1991 a new group, <u>Oregon Sportsmen's Defense Fund, Inc.</u>, was formed for the specific purpose of uniting all of the efforts of Oregon's sportsmen and the various groups they belong to in order to ensure that sportsmen's interests are capably and fairly represented in the political process here in Oregon. The OSDF philosophical statement on its newsletter, "Oregon Sportsmen Protecting Our Heritage Through Unity" summarizes the group's purpose well.

I am in my second year of membership in OSDF, and I have been extremely impressed with the level of accountability maintained between the group's leadership and its membership. Truly OSDF represents each sportsmen's interests.

OSDF's tireless effort in the Oregon Legislative Session in 1993 is the only reason that sportsmen were not sorely surprised when the new hunting regulations came out this year. Furthermore, OSDF's continued membership growth and its presence in the polical process is paramount to Oregon sportsmen's future rights and opportunities to hunt, trap and own guns. OSDF keeps its membership up to date on which legislators represent sportsmen's interests and on what bills are being discussed in the legislature and behind the scenes. Any Oregon outdoorsman who is not a member of OSDF is missing his best opportunity to do his part in the sportsmen's effort and to be kept abreast of all the news and political developments-- and threats-- related to his favorite pastime. Certainly each state would do well to have a united state sportsmen's group like OSDF.

If you are an Oregonian, or if you are from another state but interested in possibly starting a similar united sportsmen's group in your state, and would like more information about the OSDF, write to Oregon Sportsmen's Defense Fund, PO Box 100, Blachly, Oregon 97412; phone 503-925-3022.

The time for active involvement by every outdoorsman in the political process is right now. We must not continue to count on someone else to do all the work in preserving our rights. Hunting's future and every citizen's future right to "keep and bear arms" is dependent on each person taking the initiative now to become involved in the political process. Tomorrow, literally, may be too late!

# Index

<u>Blacktail Deer Hunting Adventures</u> is the ***perfect gift*** for your deer hunting friends. For more copies see next page...

# Ordering  Information

For additional copies of <u>Blacktail Deer Hunting Adventures</u>
send check or money order to :

**Lost Creek Books**
**P.O. Box 50185**
**Eugene, Or 97405**

| Unit Cost | Number of Copies | Ext. Price |
|---|---|---|
| $12.95 | | |
| Shipping | | $2.50 |
| Total Enclosed | | |

# Ordering  Information

For additional copies of <u>Blacktail Deer Hunting Adventures</u>
send check or money order to :

**Lost Creek Books**
**P.O. Box 50185**
**Eugene, Or 97405**

| Unit Cost | Number of Copies | Ext. Price |
|---|---|---|
| $12.95 | | |
| Shipping | | $2.50 |
| Total Enclosed | | |